Unraveling The Universal Life Scam

Richard Proteau

Editor: Alison Proteau

ISBN:1503246167
ISBN-13:9781503246164

"Praise for Richard Proteau' Shorter Truth which takes the myth and magic out of financial planning!"

After a 3 year investigation, Richard Proteau reveals the scam behind the Universal Life:

On June 16th 2004, the Canadian Institute of Actuaries held a conference on Managing Universal Life moderated by Stephen T. Krupicz of Manulife with Scott G. Sadler and Promod K. Sharma as speakers. Unbelievably in the proceedings of this conference, the actuaries discussed how they were deceiving consumers in buying Universal life by producing fraudulent illustrations:

"And then there are also detriments in the design which work against the consumer acceptance and an example of that would be high management expense ratios (MERs). Insurance companies are not typically seen as the place to go if you have money to invest, and the high MERs that companies offer are an example in the consumer's mind of being out of touch. Now we know why the MERs are high - it is because of the bonuses that are paid to help the illustrations look good. So if you are able to provide a 1.2% bonus with an MER of three percent, if you wanted to have a higher bonus say 1.5%, you just increase the MER by a corresponding amount - smoke and mirrors. Now the reason this works is that when comparisons are run they are usually at the same projected interest rate, so differences in MERs are ignored, and differences in crediting practices are also ignored."

Those who sell you Universal Life don't even believe in what they are presenting you! Ron Atkinson Vice-President & Marketing Actuary PPI Financial Group:

"Unfortunately as you will see, today's illustrations reflect very little of the reality of how a policy will actually perform in the future."

What is the Financial Services Commission of Ontario says about all of this deception:

"On July 14, 2013, you sent me an e-mail pertaining to the use of constant interest rates in Life Insurance Illustrations and how these affect the future values of universal policies. You feel this constitutes an Unfair and Deceptive Act or Practice under Ontario Regulation 07/00. Based on the evidence you have provided, we cannot conclude that these parameters are in and of themselves unfair or deceptive, as each case must be considered on its own merits. You asked for a disclaimer to be added to these illustrations. You may wish to raise your concerns with the CLHIA. Bien à vous, Manon Azar Compliance Officer FSCO"

These actuaries and agents break their own code of ethics towards consumers as reflected in the principles of CLHIA's Consumer Code of Ethics including:

"To ensure that Illustrations of prices, values and benefits are clear and fair, and contain appropriate disclosure of amounts which are not guaranteed." and
"To advertise products and services clearly and straightforwardly, and to avoid practices which might mislead or deceive."

WE NEED YOUR HELP!!!

If you have owned or currently own a Universal Life policy, you can help the Financial Services Consumer Alliance (FSCA) recover hundreds of millions of dollars in illicit profits taken by insurers from millions of consumers who have purchased this product.

WE ARE NOT ASKING FOR MONEY! WE ARE JUST ASKING FOR A LITTLE BIT OF YOUR TIME!!!

The objective of FSCA is to talk to 1000 consumers who have or had a Universal Life product to gather important data that will help in properly structuring the future Class Action associated with this product.

We need data about the illustrations that were shown to you such as interest rate used, investment option used, premium period payment, cash values at different durations versus present values…

This data will make the Class Action more efficient and in the end, it will mean more money in your pocket…

Take the first step by filling the preliminary form at

http://www.consumerights.ca/database.html

CONTENTS

To Benoit and Cameron

Every time I look at you I am reminded that the differences between right and wrong do matter; that the truth, whether big or small is worth fighting for.

FOREWORD

Should you consider buying a Universal Life as an investment? The answer is pretty simple and it is "Never." Keep investment separate from insurance and your financial plan will look a lot better.

WARNING: This statement does not condemn permanent insurance or the decision of prepaying permanent insurance. This statement condemns a product that was designed as an impossible investment and sold to deliver "smoke and mirrors" results.

The objective of the Shorter Truth Series is to get myths and magic out of the information relating to financial decisions. In the first book, we tackle the myth of the Universal Life as an investment. The Shorter Truth is written using layman's terms as there are more than enough nebulous terms found in Universal Life contracts. This also applies to the decision of minimizing the use of mathematics as there are enough fool's numbers found on illustrations. In 100 pages or less, I will teach you why people should not buy a Universal Life as an investment. If you have bought a Universal Life policy in the past, it may be possible to save the viability of your financial purchase. These pages will tell you what you need to do in order to protect your rights, because insurers are conspiring to prevent you from taking advantage of the Universal Life you purchased.

This book is endorsed by the Financial Consumer Service Alliance:

"Truth and honesty are the best forms of advice. In this book, Richard Proteau delivers plenty of both. Anyone considering buying permanent life insurance as an investment should listen to what he has to say.".

DEMUTUALIZATION

"Was the demutualization the result of the expropriation of the capital by senior managers for their own benefits? Having lived through different demutualization, I have observed no proof or evidence of this. This expropriation came in fact much later, after demutualization, demonstrating that greed is like a seed. When it was watered by demutualization, it was only a question of time before human nature followed its course." (Richard Proteau 2013)

It is strange to start our analysis of the Universal Life by talking about demutualization. However, there is a certain logic to this approach.

Demutualization drastically changed the insurance industry. Traditionally, the business of the insurer was to accept unpredictable risks that third parties were unwilling to assume in exchange for a premium. This form of risk management, used to hedge against the risk of a contingent and uncertain loss, was very important to the development of all nations' economies.

Insurance involves pooling funds from many insured to pay for the losses that a few of these insured may incur. The insured are protected from risk by paying a premium, with the premium being dependent upon the frequency and severity of the insured risk. I have always found that insurance is noble because of this element. It demonstrates the best form of capitalism is achieved by reaching a balance between competition and collaboration.

Insurance was provided by mutual insurance companies owned entirely by its policyholders. Therefore, in the design and pricing of the products, there was always a correlation between the needs of its current and future policyholders and the objectives of the insurer. By being limited to raising capital through its policyholders, mutual insurance companies were forced to adopt long term financial goals. This is not an easy task for mutual companies. It is a constant balancing act in having to match the high acquisition cost of life insurance and the capital required to fund policy reserves against long term profits. The greater the success a mutual insurance company has with sales, it results in less capital since capital is depleted in order to provide the reserves mandated to be set aside against each individual policy sold. This practice limits the mutual company's growth to the limit of “responsible growth”.

Then came the emergence of the global economy, where bigger is always better. The public was convinced that mutual insurance companies had to grow outside of the limit of responsible growth. The only way to do this was for the mutual companies to become stock companies owned by investors. Responsible growth had to be removed to increase short term profits. Under this new structure, capital is provided through the issue of stocks and any profits generated by a stock insurance company are distributed to the investors without necessarily benefiting the policyholders.

Demutualization is the process by which a customer-owned mutual organization changes its legal form to become a joint stock company. Demutualization allows a broader capital base but there is now a mismatch of expectations. The shareholder wants short term profits which cannot be delivered by the taking of risks through the selling of insurance products. Short term profits will need to be subsidized through unethical and even fraudulent commercial practices such as a decline in customer service, misleading marketing and practices, or refusal to pay claims. Risk management becomes a costly expense and will be overlooked. The best example of this practice is the decision by Manulife to not reinsure the guarantees of its segregated funds: *“In the early 2000s, D'Alessandro convinced Manulife's board and executives that it was no longer necessary to take out costly hedges to backstop the guarantees in its variable-rate annuities and segregated funds. Then stock markets around the world crashed by 50% in 2008-09, and Manulife's capital levels sank. As of today, Manulife and Sun Life are still setting aside large amounts to bolster their reserves, and often taking quarterly hits of several hundred million dollars to account for revised actuarial assumptions."* (1)

Shareholders don't like reserves and therefore don't like insurance sales because it eats up capital and reduces their dividend yield. This is a source of great frustration for CEOs of stock insurance companies, as reported by the Globe and Mail in regards to Manulife: *"Guloien was clearly frustrated. In response to a question, he noted that some competing U.S. companies were increasing dividends and buying back stock to boost shareholder value, but IFRS still required him to bolster his capital. "It is what it is. We don't have roller skates," he said."*(2)

So what does it all mean to you as a consumer?

It means that it will become increasingly difficult for you to find and buy insurance products that offer any real value because insurers don't want to insure risks. This is summarized by a reinsurer, Swiss Re: *"Originally, risk protection – providing a benefit after a specific event, such a death – was the focus and main value of life insurers. Today most life insurers consider their main core competency to be managed retirement savings. Life insurers have become long-term assets managers."*(3)

It means that insurers still wanting to offer life insurance will design products to insure risk while returning this risk back to the insured without his knowledge. As a result, the marketing and sales practices of these products will become deceptive. This is what has happened with the Universal Life product.

It means that consumers need to find a way to make their purchase efficient. The low interest environment currently existing has enhanced the value of past Universal Life policies while decreasing the value of Universal Life policies that will be purchased in the future. Insurers will do anything to prevent consumers from taking advantage of the value created by this low interest environment for past purchased Universal Life policies. Denial of service and information will be used by insurers to force policy holders to lapse their Universal Life with a low cost of insurance based on high interest rates.

Finally, it means that Insurers will start introducing adjustable insurance products which will provide the insurer the contractual discretion to adjust its acceptance of risk throughout the life of the contract, based on its profit expectations, at the expense of the insured.

Based on the deceptive sale practices used to increase Universal Life policy sales, we can expect that consumers will also be misled in regards to these adjustable insurance products. This will be the subject of another book in The Shorter Truth series. Unraveling the Universal Life Scam is about what to do with your existing Universal Life policy, and why not to buy new Universal Life policies as investment.

RULE #1: In buying an insurance product, never accept a risk that an insurer is unwilling to take because it has deemed that risk to be unprofitable.

(1) (2) Big Insurance worries about the future JOHN DALY The Globe and Mail Published Thursday, Jun. 28 2012,
(3) Swiss Re Sigma no 4.Nov 2004 Mortality Protection: the core of life.

BUYING FROM A MUTUAL INSURANCE COMPANY

"The value of a financial product purchase consists not solely in the near equality of price and benefits. It must include the consideration of mutual trust." (Richard Proteau)

There are still some mutual insurance companies operating in Canada. Before talking about Universal Life, I wanted to answer this question: "Are there any advantages to buying insurance from a mutual company rather than a stock company?"

Permanent insurance is an important product that offers a lot of value for those who need or want it. Permanent insurance should be simple and guaranteed, which Universal Life is not. Insurance should never be considered as an investment vehicle.

If you are buying a permanent insurance product, such as whole life or a simplified Universal Life (ie; Term 100 with guaranteed investments to prepay cost of insurance), should you buy such a product through a stock company or through a mutual company? The answer while simple becomes a question. Which one do you trust?

If you are buying permanent insurance, you are investing into a long term contract with long term objectives. The customer's objectives should coincide with the insurer's objectives. This is why stock companies are not the best at offering permanent insurance. If you require permanent insurance, I would strongly recommend that you purchase from a mutual company because as a policyholder you are an owner of the company.

As a policyholder and owner of the company, if financial variables used in the pricing of your life insurance were too optimistic, you would be neutral about this since it means that, while you will be receiving less dividends, your policy is now more valuable. If you are a stockholder, this is not the case and a stockholder will do anything to preserve profits.

If the mutual company forgets its culture, this is the first step towards demutualization. Should demutualization happen, your financial purchase will allow you to receive compensation through the receipt of shares of the new stock company. This can go a long way towards making your financial purchase a profitable one. Aside from niche mutual companies, the two most important mutual companies are Equitable Life, and Assumption life. Strong consideration should be given to these two companies in your purchase of permanent insurance.

Rule#2: Only buy a financial product from those companies that operate on the same time horizon as you do.

THE VANISHING PREMIUM SCANDAL

"The roots of the Universal Life scam lie deep in the insurance industry's culture and nature; unwilling and unable to change, it is condemned to commit its original sin over and over again…" (Richard Proteau)

To understand that Universal Life is a scam, one must understand the Original Sin of the life insurance industry; the 'vanishing premium' sales concept.

When Universal Life was introduced in the late 1970s, it revolutionized the insurance industry by unbundling the insurance from its savings element. However, this sparked a war against traditional insurance products and many insurers modified their whole life products to compete against Universal Life products. This is described by Richard T. Phillips, of the law firm Smith and Phillips, who was very involved in litigation surrounding the 'vanishing premiums' sale concept:

"These products involved complex combinations of whole life insurance, term insurance, and paid-up additions in proportions allowing favorable premium levels and adjustable face amounts. Policy dividends, additional premiums, and "dump ins" were all used to purchase paid-up insurance that would offset the temporary term coverage."(4)

These complex new products were all interest sensitive and were sold through the use of computer-generated "sales illustrations" produced by Head Office employees.

"Vanishing premium was one of the most aggressive techniques used to sell the new products. Employing complex actuarial techniques, the computer-generated sales illustrations of the vanishing premium companies illustrated how a customer could "roll over" his cash value from an existing policy, or make only a limited number of premium payments, in some cases as few as four. Based upon the assumptions (frequently undisclosed) employed in the illustration software, the premium would "vanish" and no further cash outlay would be due."(5)

In the settlement of the litigation no insurers admitted their guilt. This meant that the employees who had been involved with creating and promoting this sales strategy remained in their positions and were not held accountable for their actions. The guilt of the insurers and their employees was not a question of doubts. It was proven in different individual lawsuits such as Ward against Manulife where a judge of the Superior Court of Ontario found that:

"[27] The agents were provided with computer-generated documentation that appeared to confirm the reasons for the optimism. These projections were quite sophisticated and were the result of work by actuaries and other professionals at head office. The Wards, like other agents, were not the authors of this optimism nor were they advised about the details leading to the justification for it."(6)

The end of litigation of vanishing premiums, resulting in multi-million dollar class action settlements, led to changes to the very foundation of the life insurance industry. The public believed that this type of practice would never occur again. An important lesson was about to be learned. The lesson? That the culture of an industry is as important as the way transactions are done.

After the demise of the discredited Whole Life product, Universal Life began its supreme reign in the market. Competition for sales became intense again and it was not long before the same employees involved with the vanishing premium introduced deceptive sales practices to make their Universal Life product illustrations appear more valuable than the products truly were.

Sales practices began to revolve around how to artificially increase cash values appearing on illustrations without informing the consumer of the risk he was taking or, that it would be impossible for him to achieve the results that had been illustrated. This started the cash values war.

These employees involved with vanishing premium had learned a lesson. They learned to protect themselves against civil litigation , and so they introduced three important changes in order to ensure that consumers could not hold them accountable for their new deceptive sales practices.

First, they changed the agent contract to make them independent, even creating an intermediary (MGA) between the company and the agent. Second, they made certain that illustrations were produced by the agent and not Head Office. Finally, they introduced an 'interest sensitivity ' page that stated that the purchaser of the Universal Life understood that the illustrations were not guaranteed. This page would have to be signed by the client with the goal of absolving the company employees of any guilt in creating false expectations through their "fraudulent" illustrations.

Empowered by these changes, the insurers were ready to turn legitimate sales of Universal Life into a scam by promoting it as a tax sheltered investment.

It is worthwhile to note the words of Richard Phillips as a closing comment on the vanishing premium, and sales of Universal Life.

RULE#3: Nothing vanishes in financial planning; most of all deception.

(4)(5)"VANISHING PREMIUM" LITIGATION: The Plaintiffs' Perspective by Richard T. Phillips 1996
(6) Ward against Manulife PICTON COURT FILE NO.: 00-CV-14495 DATE: 2006/06/

July 10, 2014
Via E-mail & U.S. Mail
rproteau@consumerights.ca

Richard Proteau, President
Financial Services Consumer Alliance
457 Nelson St.
New Glasgo, NS B2H3C4
Canada

RE: Vanishing Premium

Dear Richard:

Thank you for your e-mail received yesterday. I am glad to learn of your organization to help insurance policyholders in Canada. In response to your inquiry about the vanishing premium litigation, and the subsequent events in Canada and the U.S., I would say the following:

Civil litigation in the United States - and I suspect in Canada as well - as a practical matter is able to serve only three purposes: (1) to obtain recompense, to the extent possible, for the victims of wrongdoing such as that described in your email, (2) to punish the corporate wrongdoer for its actions (to the extent a financial penalty can do so), and (3) to serve as a deterrent to prevent the wrongdoer and similarly situated companies from engaging in the wrongful practices in the future. What civil litigation cannot do - and likely will never be able to do - is prevent innovative corporate and individual wrongdoers from *constantly coming up* with novel new ways to take advantage of policyholders and other consumers in their dealings.

The decade of vanishing premium litigation throughout the United States, from about 1994 through 2004, did yield the results and produce the benefits intended in the civil justice system. Through individual litigation, initially, and subsequently class actions, policyholders nationwide obtained, to the extent possible, at least partial recompense for the harm caused by the life insurance companies' wrongful illustration and sales practices. The financial bite and adverse publicity of punitive damage awards caused life insurers to change the practices that had given rise to the litigation.

What did not change was the creativity of the defendant companies. It was not long before new approaches were devised to increase profits at the expense of policyholders. I am involved right now in investigating a "bonus illustration" scheme similar to the one discussed in your email. As with the vanishing premium cases, successfully combating these new practices in the civil justice system will require a creative approach by policyholders' attorneys. Hopefully the actions by policyholder attorneys here in the U.S. will again be of benefit to those in Canada.

Post Office Drawer 1586
Batesville, MS 38606

RICHARD T. PHILLIPS
662-563-4613
flip@smithphillips.com
Fax 662-563-1546

Smith Phillips Building
695 Shamrock Drive
Batesville, MS 38606

SMITH, PHILLIPS, MITCHELL, SCOTT & NOWAK, LLP, ATTORNEYS AT LAW
BATESVILLE & HERNANDO
MISSISSIPPI
www.smithphillips.com

Richard Proteau, President
July 10, 2014
Page 2

Via E-Mail & U.S. Mail

One thing is certain: Neither Financial Services Consumer Alliance in Canada, nor United Policyholders in the U.S., need worry about becoming *irrelevant* ! The business practices of ever-growing national and multi-national financial and insurance corporations makes your efforts – and those of policyholder attorneys addressing these issues in the 21st Century – more and more important to society.

Thank you for your email. If I may be of help to you, or any of your members, in any way please let me know.

Sincerely,

Richard T. Phillips

RTP:nm
cc: Amy Bach, United Policyholders
amy@unitedpolicyholders.org
David Baria, Esq.
dbaria@baria-williamsom.com

THE HISTORY OF UNIVERSAL LIFE AND BEGINNING OF THE CASH VALUE WARS

"Like vanishing premium, the universal life scam is the result of a culture of cheating. It was wrong for us to think we could implement changes without changing the culture." (Richard Proteau)

G.R. Dinney was the first to predict the rise of the Universal Life when he addressed the Canadian Institute of Actuaries in 1971. His presentation entitled "A Descent into the Maelstrom of the Insurance Future," was followed in 1975 by articles by James C.H. Anderson, president of Tillinghast & Company where Anderson further defined "The Universal Life Insurance Policy". This new product would combine two unbundled elements, term life insurance and an accumulation fund, controlled and managed by the policyholder.

Under the terms of the policy, the premium payments less the premium tax are credited to the cash value of the policy. The cash value is credited each month with interest. The policy is debited each month by a cost of insurance (COI), as well as any other policy charges and fees which are drawn from the cash value, even if no premium payments are made.

It was believed that Universal Life's lower per-dollar commission would lead to a restructuring of the distribution system, with greater efficiency and lower cost to the investor. This did not take place, because companies effectively transferred the existing compensation of Whole Life to the Universal Life.

The massive increase in Universal Life sales through 1985 was the result of interest rates credited on Universal Life products. These interest rates were significantly higher than the yield of traditional life products. High interest rates made Universal Life attractive as a replacement, and sales of UL started to cannibalize blocks of business made up of traditional life products.

To this point, Universal Life had been pretty simple in design and therefore not susceptible to deception. When interest rates tapered off and the stock market took off, insurers decided to provide investments linked to various stock indexes. It is important to understand that to this point, insurance was usually not viewed as an investment. Insurers competed on premiums paid, versus insurance obtained.

The addition of index linked accounts changed everything by introducing an incomparable level of complexity to Universal Life, by changing the focus from insurance to cash values, and positioning insurance as an investment. This complexity, which could not be readily understood by consumers, enabled the insurer to bundle the insurance element with the investment element once again. This was done by using incomprehensible Management Expense Ratios (MER). These ratios were used to subsidize the cost of insurance without the consumer's knowledge.

At the same time, an important change to the distribution of insurance was taking place. A new addition to the distribution of life insurance was emerging. It was the National Accounts and this involved firms such as Wood Gundy, Merryl Lynch... This new distribution channel sparked a war between insurers for the domination of this new channel. The munitions used were the cash values appearing on illustrations. Quickly, this war of cash values spread to all distribution channels.

Rule#4: Never buy a complex financial product where the insurer designed the product on the assumption that the policyholder will receive inadequate service.

INDEX LINK ACCOUNTS AND UNIVERSAL LIFE

"Any cheater can make permanent life insurance complex to allow the use of deceit in order to increase sales. It takes a special person to move against this trend because he believes that selling permanent insurance should be simple and straightforward." (Richard Proteau)

The investment options within a Universal Life product used to be relatively simple and straightforward and, as a result it, was extremely difficult to deceive the consumer. The objective was also simple which was to pay the policy as efficiently as possible. Investments were usually of a fixed term or GIC in nature with a minimum interest guarantee of 4% which would make these contracts very valuable on a fair market value basis later on. Everything changed when fixed interest rates dropped to their currently record low levels while returns available on equity investments soared to record highs.

Universal Life then began to be positioned as an investment opportunity in order to compete for the consumer's savings dollars. In fact, some insurance companies were not satisfied with this and tried to create a Universal Life that could compete directly with mutual funds which was impossible to do when you consider commission (190% of premium for UL versus 5% of premium for a mutual fund) and the cost of insurance.

This meant that insurers had to make their illustrations look good. They had the perfect opportunity to do this with the addition of new investment options linked to stock indexes.

These indexes could be anything from the TSE 100, the S&P 500, Morgan Stanley world index, etc.. Using existing mutual funds offered by companies like AGF or Trimark introduced the ability for the insurers to double up on Management Expense Ratios (MER).

Insurers could have kept the introduction of Index Linked funds simple by adopting standards and by preventing the application of double MERs through a simple MER formula such as the Total Return Index less 3%. Instead, the insurers introduced MER formulas that even someone with a doctorate in mathematics would not be able to understand and estimate. This was crucial for actuaries if they wanted to make their illustrations as deceptive as possible.

The first layer of complexity was the introduction of MER based on the Price Index instead of the Total Index. The Price Index represents the value of the Total Index, less the value of the dividends. Based on historical records, the average value of these dividends represents a 3.5% MER. However this is an average figure because dividends vary every year. With this formula the insurer was able to introduce variable MERs.

In a lot of Universal Life, the insurer could also take an additional charge off the Price Index yields. This meant a double MER would not be apparent to the consumer , with said double MER reaching as high as 6%. Double MER also applied to Index funds linked to mutual funds such as Trimark, where the insurer would apply an MER of 3%+ on top of the MER applied by Trimark.

This level of complexity was not enough for certain insurers. Some companies created an MER formula impossible to estimate or comprehend by using a percentage of the gain or losses associated with an Index. The MER would therefore vary significantly based on the variation of the changes. It's not surprising that such changes were tallied on a daily basis with the net effect of multiplying the

MER, as shown by Ron Atkinson Vice-President & Marketing Actuary PPI Financial Group:

"In 1996 the TSE 35 total return index increased by 30%. A 10% margin applied to the annual change would give the company a 3% spread.

The total of the monthly changes up and down for the TSE 35 total return index in 1996 however were 52%. So a 10% margin applied monthly now gives the company a 5.2% spread, that's almost double.

The daily figures give a total of all the changes of 125% for a total spread to the company over the year of 12.5%, about 4 times the annual figure. Fortunately this type of linkage formula has largely disappeared but it was quite common in up until a about a year ago and there are still some products that use this approach." (7)

Would you buy an investment with a 12.5% MER? Who would consider buying such Universal Life unless he has been deceived? Who would design such product unless his main objective is deception?

Finally, other invisible costs can increase the MER further, such as the currency risk if you have selected the S&P 500.

It is important to note that most advisors use only the illustration to sell a Universal Life product. The advisor's client is usually not offered a sample contract to help him understand the policy he is buying . Most advisors don't present the marketing materials created by the insurers either. As a result, most consumers get their policy contract when the policy is issued which can be months after the illustration was shown.

Illustrations sell life insurance and actuaries know this. This makes the perfect opportunity to capitalize on impossible cash values in order to promote the sales of Universal Life as an investment.

RULE 6: If it's too hard to understand as a product, it should be too hard to buy the product.

(7) http://www.hatton.ca

THE UNIVERSAL LIFE AND THE ART OF DECEPTION

"Pay no attention to the numbers behind a Universal Life illustration as it is built upon deception after deception." (Richard Proteau)

At one point in my career I worked for Maritime Life. I was in charge of a team responsible for the competitive analysis of Universal Life. Unhappy with simply comparing illustrations, as it does not provide a picture of the reality, I adapted statistical sciences to create correlation factors. These factors would indicate the degree of correlation between illustrated cash values and probable cash values. While I don't use these factors in this book, I do mention it to reassure you that my conclusions are supported by mathematics.

The First Deception: Using net rate of returns

Let's look at two illustrations wherein a client plans to invest $2000 per year in a Universal Life product with an 8% rate of return. Remember, these are illustrations.

		Company A		Company B	
Year	Premium	COI	CSV	COI	CSV
10	2,000	1,000	15,645	950	16,427
20	2,000	1,000	49,422	950	51,894
30	2,000	1,000	122,345	950	128,463
40	2,000	1,000	279,781	950	293,770

COI: Cost of insurance, CSV: Cash Surrender Value

Based on these results, it is easy to decide which company is offering the best product. However the 8% is net of the MERs. Are the MERs the same for both companies? The answer is "no". What the illustrations do not provide is the fact that Company A has an MER of 3% and Company B has an MER of 3.5%. Assuming a gross return of 11%, Company A net return would be 8% and Company B would be 7.5%. (Note how MER subsidizes the cost of insurance and how Universal Life is not unbundled anymore.) Using these more accurate rates of returns, we get the following illustrations:

		Company A(11%/8%)		Company B(11%/7.5%)	
Year	Premium	COI	CSV	COI	CSV
10	2,000	1,000	15,645	950	15,968
20	2,000	1,000	49,422	950	48,880
30	2,000	1,000	122,345	950	116,712
40	2,000	1,000	279,781	950	256,515

Note: Imagine for a moment that company B was using an Index link mutual fund with double MERs and total MER of 6%, the real rate of return would have been reduced to 5%. MER is the most important factor behind illustrated cash values, and they are not reflected in illustrations.

As we can see, the picture changes drastically with Company A now being the favorite. Company A could promote the fact that its MERs are better by telling agents to run illustration comparisons between the two companies by using the adjusted net rate of returns. However, from past experience I can tell you that advisors refuse to use different rates of returns for different companies because they don't want to have to explain or disclose the differences in MERs. Company A must therefore find a way to increase the illustrated values without really changing anything. This is done through the investment bonus found in Universal Life.

The second level of deception: Bonus in Universal Life

So Company A, knowing that the advisors won't disclose the MERs and won't do different illustrations for different MERs, decides to use a "bonus" to artificially increase its illustrated cash values. The company decides to offer a 1% bonus by increasing its MER to 4%. The net MER for Company A still remains 3% (4% MER less 1% bonus). However, now the effective illustration rate of Company A increases to 9% (8% net illustration rate + 1% bonus). The new illustrated values for Company A become:

		Company A (8% with bonus/9%)		Company B (8%)	
Year	Premium	COI	CSV	COI	CSV
10	2,000	1,000	16,560	950	16,427
20	2,000	1,000	55,674	950	51,894
30	2,000	1,000	148,575	950	128,463
40	2,000	1,000	368,291	950	293,770

A client seeing this would say "Wow! Company A rocks!!!" and would be deceived into buying the Universal Life of Company A. Buying without knowing that the illustrated values of Company A do not reflect the increase of the MER from 3% to 4%. This hidden increase in the real world (but not on the illustration) negates the impact of the "bonus", which had brought the illustration's rate up to 9%. It is quite the sleight of hand! This is what actuaries refer to as "smoke and mirrors results". As a result of this magic trick, the probability of reaching the illustrated results is reduced to nothing. Also the results are now conditional on 12% gross rate of return in order to achieve an 8% net return. This is a tremendous increase in volatility and risk that the client is not seeing on the illustration. This technique of deception used to overstate cash values of an illustration is discussed by actuaries at a conference of the Canadian Society of Actuaries:

"And then there are also detriments in the design which work against the consumer acceptance and an example of that would be high management expense ratios (MERs). Insurance companies are not typically seen as the place to go if you have money to invest, and the high MERs that companies offer are an example in the consumer's mind of being out of touch. Now we know why the MERs are high - it is because of the bonuses that are paid to help the illustrations look good. So if you are able to provide a 1.2% bonus with an MER of three percent, if you wanted to have a higher bonus say 1.5%, you just increase the MER by a corresponding amount - smoke and mirrors. Now the reason this works is that when comparisons are run they are usually at the same

projected interest rate, so differences in MERs are ignored, and differences in crediting practices are also ignored." (8)

The third level of deception: The conditional bonus

Company B won't go down without a fight. It could introduce a bonus of 1% as Company A did, but you can only increase the MER so much and have it remain unnoticed. A 4.75% MER would be too steep. So it decides to increase its MER to 4% and match company A and also to offer a bonus of 1%. However, there is one new caveat. The bonus is conditional on earning an 8% net rate of return

		Company A (8% with bonus/9%)		Company B (8%+ cond. bonus/9%)	
Year	Premium	COI	CSV	COI	CSV
10	2,000	1,000	16,560	950	17,388
20	2,000	1,000	55,674	950	58,522
30	2,000	1,000	148,575	950	156,004
40	2,000	1,000	368,291	950	386,706

How can Company B offer a bonus of 1% if it only increases its MER by .25% to 4%? This would create a shortfall of .75% . It's a pretty simple trick.

The bonus is conditional on getting a credited rate of 8% and therefore earning a gross rate of 12%. On the illustration, because we are using a constant rate of return of 8%, it is assumed that this conditional bonus is credited 100% of the time. In reality, the rate of return will fluctuate above and below 12%. The question is, by how much? In this case, it was assumed that the bonus would be credited only 25% of the time. Therefore its value is really .25% and not 1%. Since this important information is not shown on the illustration, the buyer is fooled in thinking Company B product is better because it offers what seems to be better cash values.

NOTE: In both cases, the use of a bonus has allowed both companies to artificially increase the case values at duration 40

by more than $100,000.

The Fourth level of deception: Constant rate of return

Illustrations based on index link funds are done using a constant rate of return when the returns of these investments are actually volatile and change from year to year. As a result, the illustration does not show the impact that volatility can have on cash values.

Before we get deeper into this subject, I do have to go over some very simple mathematics. First, in a static financial system where there are no exits and no entries of money, the sequence of returns does not impact the final cash value at the end of the sequence.

Let's say you have $1,000 invested. You will have the same amount of money if you make 6% in year 1, 8% in year 2 and 10% in year 3 than if you make 10% in year 1, 8% in year 2 and 6% in year 3. This is called the Commutative Law of Multiplication. Also these 2 sequences of return result in an average rate of 8% and would give you about the same amount of money had you earned a constant 8% rate of return for those 3 years.

If life insurance was based on a single premium payment, and no charges were deducted, this would be the only time a constant rate of return would correlate with any volatile returns with the same average rate .

The commutative law ceases to apply when money is added or subtracted from the system. For example, the commutative law would not apply if you paid a $1,000 premium every year, with a cost of insurance of $500 deducted from the policy each year. The cash value at the end of the first sequence (6%,8%,10%) would be very different than the cash value resulting from the second sequence (10%,8%,6%).

In this situation, the illustrated values shown for a constant rate of return of 8% will differ significantly from the values resulting from each individual possible sequence of volatile returns based on an average 8% return.

It has been proven that 2 investments yielding the same average rate of return and rate of withdrawal, but with 2 different rates of volatility (with Company A's policy investment varying from -1% to 13% while Company B's policy investment varies between -7% and 19%), can result in up to 50% less cash values over a 30 year period. If we were to compare these results against an illustration with a constant rate of return, it gets a lot worse. (9)

Therefore, when an illustration is done using a constant rate of return for a volatile investment, illustrated values versus real values based will be overstated by as much as 100%. This overstatement of illustrated values increases with time and with the constant rate of return used.

The shorter truth is simple. Illustrations done using a constant rate of return are a lie for Index Link Universal Life policies.

The fifth level of deception: High constant rate of return

Let's forget mathematics for a moment and just use common sense. Thibault was an advisor in Quebec who defrauded many clients in that province. This criminal used all of the levels of deception described above in order to make his illustrations look good. On top of this, he added a new level of deception to create product illustrations that his clients could not resist.

The fifth level of deception Thibault used (and which was allowed by the insurer, AIG Canada) was to apply a constant rate of return of 11.45%. Factoring the MER, this meant the client had to earn 15% each year for the life of the policy to get the illustrated cash values. I don't want to go into the mathematics and use standard deviation to make my argument, so l will keep it simple.

Rates of return don't vary without a limit. Let's assume rates vary between 25% and -25%. If the clients earned 25% in the first year, this would be 10% above the assumed 15% constant rate of return and the client would be 10% ahead of the illustration. If the client earns -25%, this would be 40% below the assumed 15% constant rate of return. To recover the ground lost, the client would have to earn 25% each year for 4 years, which is impossible. The 15% constant rate of return is simply a lie and a fraud.

The software of insurers should not allow the use of such of constant rate of return for volatile investments. If the software is unable to illustrate volatile rate of returns, then the constant rate of return must be kept low so that a correlation can exist between what is illustrated and what is possible. This maximum constant rate of return is 5%, and I would even suggest 4%.

Anyone who has been shown a constant rate of return above 5% for a volatile investment has been deceived by the insurer and by his advisor.

Rule#7: Never rely on a Universal Life illustration, unless it is guaranteed, because what is shown is probably just a scam.

(8) Proceedings of the Canadian Institute of Actuaries, Vol. XXXV, No. 2, June 2004
(9)http://www.michaelpace.net/pdfs/Volatility_Impact_During_Withdrawals.pdf

THE SIGNED INTEREST SENSIBILITY PAGE: IS IT AN AUTHORIZATION TO DECEIVE?

For insurers profits are sweet even if they come from deception (an adaptation of Sophocles quote)

Scenario: You realize that you did not buy an insurance product but instead bought an illustration based upon deceit. You've found out why your actual cash values are very different than your illustrated values and this means it will cost you a lot of money to address this situation.

You have complained to the insurance company and you are considering a civil lawsuit, but you've been told that you have no chances of winning since you have signed an interest sensitivity page This signature indicates that you acknowledged knowing that rates of returns are not guaranteed and cash values are also not guaranteed since they are sensitive to actual earned rates of returns. This signature also means that you have been informed of what will happen if returns are less than illustrated; for example 1% less than illustrated returns.

Now you must ask yourself this question: "Did I sign something giving them the right to deceive me?"

The interest sensitivity page was introduced after the vanishing premium fraud to ensure that consumers understood that the results shown on an illustration were not guaranteed and that actual results could change with actual interest rates earned and credited.

This sensitivity page was designed for fixed return types of investment crediting interest rates. This sensitivity page was not updated or changed when index funds were introduced, and therefore does not educate the client about the impact of volatility on actual results. This page does not educate you about the fact that you will not get your bonus 100% of the time as illustrated (even if you earn the 8% rate of return!!) and this means that your actual cash values will be a lot less. This page does not tell you that if you earn an average rate of return of 8%, your actual cash values will still be significantly different and a lot less than the illustrated values shown to you, calculated at a constant rate of return of 8%.

Be aware that this sensitivity page does not protect the insurer from the damages done by their illustrations and software once a consumer has realized that he or she was duped into buying an illustration that was unachievable.

As a result, consumers should proceed with their complaints and should proceed with individual lawsuits or Class Actions to recover losses produced by these fraudulent illustrations.

Insurers should not be let off the hook because misled clients signed a sensitivity page that no longer serves its original intended purpose. You have never given the insurer the right to deceive you.

Rule #8: Keep insurance separate from investment; they don't mix well or not at all.

VARYING COST OF INSURANCE

"How real a Universal Life illustration is varies inversely with the number of variable involved." (Richard Proteau)

We have discussed the impact of volatile rates of return but there is also the problem of volatile costs of insurance. Not all policies have a level cost of insurance, even policies that are stated to have a level cost of insurance, and this is not something you will be shown on an illustration. Confused yet?

Cost of insurance varies with the policy's net amount of risk. So, if you start with a $1 million dollar policy and you select to have the cash value on death, the net amount at risk will remain at $1 million over the life of the policy (subject to no over funding of the policy). In other words, if you die and the policy has $250,000 cash value, the insurer will pay you the $1 million initial death benefit and the $250,000 cash value. So the insurer was at risk for $1 million and paid that amount at risk on your death. In this case only, the level cost of insurance will be indeed level.

There are policies that don't pay the cash value in addition to the death benefit. We could say that the insurer pays the cash value plus the initial face amount, less the cash value on death. As per the example above, the insurer will pay you your $250,000 cash value plus the initial death benefit of $1 million reduced by $250,000 for $750,000. So the insurer was at risk for $750,000 and paid that amount at risk on death.

In the first example, since the net amount at risk does not change, the cost of insurance will remain the same. This means if the cost of insurance selected was level, it will remain level. If the cost of insurance selected was yearly increasing, it will increase as illustrated.

In the second example, the cost of insurance will vary because the net amount at risk varies. The insurer will either apply a cost of insurance on the $750,000 or, if the cost of insurance is on $1 million, you will receive a credit for the cost of insurance associated with $250,000.

What if the cash value is not $250,000 but is instead $200,000? This means the insurer is at risk for $800,000 and would increase your cost of insurance to reflect this. As a result, the cost of insurance will be more than what was illustrated for either level or yearly increasing cost of insurance and this mean less cash values than illustrated. In this instance:

Your cost of insurance is dependent on your cash value, and your cash value is dependent on your cost of insurance. This is called negative feedback and it will send your Universal Life investment into a downward spiral.

When illustrations are done on a constant rate of return such as 8%, the cash value increases continuously which results in continuous decreases in the net amount at risk. This is on the illustration and is not what will actually happen. In reality, returns will vary from year to year and the net amount at risk will increase and decrease with the cash values. This means your cost of insurance will also vary, but you will not know this because this was not shown on the illustration.

You will not know that a higher cost of insurance due to a higher net amount at risk than was projected means less cash value. Less cash value results in an even higher net amount at risk which increases the cost of insurance further, which means a lot less cash values… I think you see what I am getting at. It is a vicious cycle and cash values will spiral downward as your cost of insurance will spiral upward. You, as a consumer, will have no idea about this since your illustration was done assuming a constant rate of return.

Can the net amount at risk be reduced by decreasing the death benefit in the bad years when the cash value is lower than expected? The easy answer is 'yes, you could'. That said, it's impossible to manage your net amount at risk because while you can reduce your death benefit by as much as you want, the law only allows you to increase it back by 8%.

For example, assume there is a drop of 20% in your cash value. You could reduce your death benefit by 20%. The next year there is a rebound in the market and your cash value increases by 20%. Now you can only increase it by 8%. This is a big problem because at this point money is pushed out of the policy creating a taxable disposition.

What if one decreases the death benefit by 8% only? This action will simply prolong the downward spiral and only means that it will take longer for your cash value to reach the bottom. As per our example, reducing your death benefit by 8% would mean your net amount at risk is still 12% too high.

Again, illustrated constant rates of return will make you believe that you are buying a pretty straight forward product, while it is anything but. This is deception at its best.

Rule #9: If you put an amount of money above the cost of insurance into a Universal Life product, your purpose should be to prepay the policy under one and only condition: "guaranteed results!"

UNIVERSAL LIFE AS A TAX SHELTER: THE GREATEST DECEPTION OF THEM ALL

"There are many hidden realities existing behind the façade of a Universal Life illustration." (Richard Proteau)

To sell Universal Life, insurers have heavily promoted the fact that funds accumulating within this product are tax exempt. Would you be surprised if this was not true?

Life insurance was virtually exempt from income tax at both the company and the policy holder level until 1968. In 1960, the government was hungry for revenues and this situation was deemed to be unfair when comparing life insurance against other investment vehicles. The Carter report was released in 1966 recommending changes to the taxation of life insurance. This report was guided by one principle; a new tax system where taxes should be imposed according to a person's ability to pay. By taxing economic power, it would have eliminated a lot of the tax avoidance strategies that exist today. The recommendation of this report in regards to life insurance was that the investment income accumulated for the benefit of the policy holder should be included in his income.

However in his 1968 budget, succumbing to a lot of pressure from the insurance industry, Finance Minister Edgar Benson did not follow the recommendation of the Carter commission. Benson introduced a hidden tax where the investment income of policy holders would be taxed in the hand of the insurance companies. It was up to these companies to find a way to transfer the cost of this tax back to the policy holder. This was a big win for insurance companies because this allowed them to continue marketing their insurance product as being tax sheltered investments.

This tax was called the Investment Income Tax (IIT) and was a 15 percent tax imposed on the taxable Canadian investment income of the insurance companies.

In 1997, it was proposed that the IIT be eliminated. Instead the government wanted to tax the investment gain in a life insurance policy upon the death of the insured in the same manner as it was taxed upon the surrender or maturity of the policy. The reaction of the insurance industry was violent. A campaign was launched using terms such as "tax on death" and the "widows' and orphans' tax". This proposal was quickly withdrawn by the federal government.

This is how it was decided that the inside build-up of the investment income of a permanent life insurance policy would not be taxed at the policy holder level. The insurers would pay this tax. The cost of this tax would then be recovered through the MER. As a result, .75% of the MER charged by the insurer is used to pay this tax.

Let's assumed the MER of the investment you have selected within your Universal Life is 3.75%, if there was no IIT, the MER would have been 3%. Are funds accumulating within a Universal Life truly tax sheltered? Absolutely not! Saying otherwise would be a lie. At most the Universal Life offers tax efficiency if you are in a marginal tax rate above 15% for a comparable investment. In this situation you would benefit from some tax deferral.

It is unbelievable to see that the federal government conspired with the insurers to hide a tax policy holders have to pay on the accumulating funds of their policies. It should be the right of any tax payers to know when they pay taxes. But it gets much worse than this. Upon surrendering their policy, the policy holder pay taxes on the cash surrender value of his policy. This is an example of double taxation because the policy holder does not get credit for the taxes he has paid.

The federal government upon the surrender of the policy does pay an IIT credit back to the insurer to avoid such double taxation since the policy holder will pay taxes on the disposition of his policy. The insurer however keeps the IIT credit and does not give it back to the policy holder. Since it is all hidden and the policy holder is unaware of this; there are no complaints.

Would you buy any investment where you will be taxed twice on your investment income? Why would you buy a Universal Life as an investment?

Rule #10: The single purpose of insurance is about you giving away risk and not about you taking on more risk.

LEVERAGING UNIVERSAL LIFE: A CONCEPT FOR THE FOOLS AND THE CHEATERS

"Leveraging thin air won't make you breathe any easier." (Richard Proteau)

It should be evident to you that the concept of leveraging a policy will not work since the values upon which this concept depends (the illustration) have nothing to do with reality.

It does not mean that the option of leveraging is bad (note the use of the word option versus the use of the word concept), but it should be your very last option when all others have failed. Leveraging is great for an 85 year old who just found out he has cancer and only has 2 to 5 years to live. At that point, the life insurance can be used as another source of funds if needed and leveraging the Universal Life would be the most efficient way to get the funds.

However, this is not how leveraging is marketed by insurers. Leveraging is marketed as a retirement strategy where the insurer will show you a beautiful illustration (that you now know is false) that depicts incredible cash values at age 65 that you will leverage at that point in time. What they don't tell you is how hard it is to manage a compounding loan over 40 years.

It is very interesting to note that the insurers, knowing that leveraging will not work when volatile rates of returns are involved, created a special concept that wealthy tax cheaters could employ. This leveraging concept was the 10/8 concept. In this concept, the insurers would offer an 8% guaranteed rate of return to the wealthy tax cheaters on the condition that they borrow the cash value at a 10% guaranteed loan rate. This shows how the insurers knew that Index funds and leveraging is the worst mix possible.

This concept guaranteed a profit of 2% for the insurer (10% loan rate less the 8% credited rate of return). The wealthy tax cheater would be able to reduce his loan rate to 5% since the interest on the loan is tax deductible and as a result he would make a guaranteed profit of 3% (8% credited rate of return less after tax 5% loan rate).

Someone always has to pay in these situations and, in this case, it is the tax payer who paid for this tax cheating arrangement at a rate of 5% (the 5% loan interest rate falsely deducted from the income of the tax cheater).

As you can see, insurers had to cheat the tax system to convince wealthy tax cheaters that leveraging was a great concept. If the wealthy could not take the risk associated with volatile rate of returns and leveraging, why would you?

Rule #11: Leveraging is a very bad investment and retirement strategy. If it is presented to you, just run away…

COMMISSION: WHAT YOU DON'T KNOW CAN HURT YOU

"The Life insurance commission bonus is the largest source of fraud and infractions committed in the life insurance industry." (Richard Proteau)

Is it surprising to you that a product sold using deception will also remunerate advisors using deception? Would you knowingly buy an investment which can pay as much as 190% of the premium in total commission to the seller? Think about this for a moment.

On a 10 year horizon, this adds up to 20% of the total funds disappearing right from the start. It will take the policy holder a minimum of 4 years to earn this 20% back. After year 6, if lucky, the policy holder will be in the money but by then only has 4 years left of the 10 years to earn any interest income above the initial amount.

Ask yourself where this 190% comes from since this is not remotely close to what an advisor has shown you.

Illustration software for Universal Life has the ability to print a commission page showing the commission which will be earned by the advisor. However this page only shows the base commission. It does not show the bonus paid on the base commission.

Most Universal Life products pay a commission of 50% to 65% of the minimum premium. This is what is shown on the commission page with the renewal commission which is usually 5% of premium paid, as well as asset based commissions of .25%.

The illustration does not show the bonus paid on this commission that can range from 100% to 205% of the base commission. If the minimum premium is $1000 and the UL pays 60% commission, the advisor will receive $600 base commission. If his bonus is 200% of the base, he will receive an additional $1,200 for a total of $1,800.

These bonuses are contingent upon a set amount of sales with a particular insurer or MGA. The amount of sales that has to be done for a 200% bonus would be around $250,000 base commission. This makes the advisor desperate to make sales. If the choices are to sell consumers a Term policy with 30% commission on a lower premium (for example $500 premium giving a base commission of $150 and a bonus of $300 for total commission of $450) ,versus a Universal Life policy with 60% commission on a much higher premium ($1,000 premium for a base commission of $600, bonus of $1,200 and total commission of $1,800), then the advisor cannot state that he is objective since there is a big conflict of interest which he is not disclosing to his client.

On top of this, there are marketing dollars and other incentives(such as trips) that are contingent on the amount of sales done by the advisor, pushing advisors to sell more Universal Life instead of term policies.

I did not mention the retro activity of bonuses. For example, if the advisor is at a bonus level of 140% but by selling you a Universal Life policy, his new level of sales ($50,000) will increase his bonus to 160%. He will therefore receive the difference between 160% and 140% for all sales he made that year (20% of $50,000 which will give him $10,000 retroactive commission) and he will lock in the 160% for the rest of the year and the following year independent of the amount of sales he will be doing. As a result, when an advisor is recommending a Universal Life policy over a Term policy, the advisor may not have your best interest at heart because he is not disclosing you all of this commission.

Why do insurers pay such high commission bonuses on Universal Life? The answer is pretty simple. Despite the higher amount of commission paid, insurers make tons of money with these sales. Let's look at an example.

A person needs a $500,000 insurance policy to protect both income and family. To purchase Term insurance, it will cost $1000. The advisor then convinces our customer of the merits of permanent insurance, and sells he or she a Universal Life policy with a $50,000 death benefit for $1000. The advisor makes more commission (60% of the premium versus 30%) and the insurer is on the hook in terms of risk for only $50,000 for the same $1000 premium. If the person dies, the insurer will have saved $450,000.

This is the reason why insurers do not ask to see the needs analysis done by advisors when an application is submitted to them , even though it is required by law . If the advisor was made to submit the needs analysis with the application, many sales of Universal Life would be prevented.

Rule #12: Always ask for a disclosure letter written by the advisor that outlines all of the base commission, bonuses and other incentives, that will be generated by your purchase of the product.

I HAVE BOUGHT A UNIVERSAL LIFE: SHOULD I SURRENDER IT?

"Illustrations are a double-edged sword. If used correctly it is a wonderful sales tool but it also makes it easier for any crappy salesman to produce extraordinary results in order to fool their potential victims." (Richard Proteau)

So, you have bought a Universal Life and you don't know what to do. First thing to do is to get a copy of the original illustration and to request an 'in force' illustration, done at a realistic rate of return. You need this in order to see what the shortfall is between what was illustrated originally, what your values are today, and what they will be tomorrow.

During the vanishing premium scandal, a funny thing happened and this was demutualization. As a result of demutualization, a lot of the policy holders who had been scammed with this vanishing premium concept received an unexpected payout of shares. Suddenly, even if they had been misled on the illustration, the value of the purchase of their policy became profitable. The same thing may have happened with your Universal Life and it's therefore important to know the fair market value (FMV) of the policy before surrendering your Universal Life.

If you purchase a Universal Life policy with an assumption of a high level of lapse, or with a cost of insurance based on high interest rate, this Universal Life policy will have a lot more value than its cash value because lapse rates and interest rates have fallen to record low levels. Also if your health has changed negatively, the FMV of your UL has increased towards the value of its death benefit.

For example, you have a UL policy with a $250,000 death benefit and with $25,000 cash value. You request a FMV evaluation to be done by an expert and you find out that your policy has an FMV of $75,000. You could donate the policy to a charity in exchange for a tax receipt of $75,000 and the tax savings would be greater than the net surrender value of the policy.

You could also sell the policy as part of a life settlement. This is why insurers are opposing life settlements. They don't want to lose money. They want you to cancel the policy at cash value so that they can get the reserves and Investment Income Tax back in addition of not paying a death benefit. This represents a lot of money in their pockets. For insurers, the purchase of a Universal Life policy should always remain unprofitable for you. This is why they are telling their agents not to reveal that your policy has a Fair Market Value that could be greater than the cash value, and they are using threats such as canceling contracts to prevent advisors from meeting their fiduciary duties to you.

Rule#13: Never accept to be under insured as a way to be able to afford permanent insurance.

DENIAL OF SERVICE

"Denying you service on Universal Life policies is part of the insurer's strategy to make your purchase unprofitable to you and thus, profitable to them." (Richard Proteau)

Ron Atkinson VP at PPI Financial stated:

"I have heard a greater number of comments lately from agents with blocks of this business that are now getting to be about 5 years old, where they are spending a great deal of time servicing the policies but are getting paid very little to do it. I know for a fact that some companies are taking this into account in their pricing.

They are assuming that with reduced or inadequate service, more policies will lapse which contributes to the lapse supported pricing I referred to earlier."(10)

Insurers are denying you service in order to increase the profitability of the Universal Life policy they have sold you. Their first strategy is to pay a lot of commission upfront, conditional on sales quotas, to influence the advisor into making the wrong recommendation by using their false illustration. As soon as the advisor has made the sale, he becomes a flight risk. He will disappear and you won't see him again and now you are responsible for the service of your own policy when you don't have the knowledge to do it.

This creates what we call orphan policies. Orphans policies are insurance policies that do not have a licensed agent to provide service. There are hundreds of thousands of these policies and their existence is one of the biggest protected secrets of the insurance industry. The other types of orphan policies are:

1) **Deceased agent**: when an agent dies, the policies he is servicing are not reassigned to a new agent. These policies become the property of the estate of the deceased agent for many years. Meanwhile, insurers are telling policy owners to contact the estate of the agent to get service on their policies... which is highly illegal...

2) **Retired agent**: when an agent retires and ceases to hold a license, the policy owners are not informed of this change. The retired agent loses access to the data of his clients and ceases to obtain notices and other information on their policies. Without access to this information service cannot be provided to policy owners and the retired agent does not have that access because, as per the law, someone who is not licensed cannot act as an agent. The insurer, even though it is against the law continues to tell the policy owner to contact the unlicensed agent to get service ... which is illegal...

3) **Numbered corporations**: A corporation cannot act as an agent because it is not a physical individual. However, many of these corporations have been created to receive the service commission paid on insurance policies. Again insurers tell the policy owner to contact these corporations to get service, which is illegal, which the policy owner cannot even do since he is unable to determine who controls the corporation.

4) **Agent whose contract is canceled for cause**: As with the retired agent, the policy owner is not informed that the agent is no

longer contracted with the insurer. This results in the agent not having access to the information on his clients, which is necessary to provide the service. Despite this fact, the insurer continues to refer the client to this agent to receive service.

5) **Agent suspended by a regulator**: When a regulator suspends an agent for a limited period or for life, the customer is not informed of this situation. The insurer continues to refer the client to the suspended agent to get service, when providing such a service would constitute a new infraction by the suspended agent.

Here is an email I wrote to Lester Heldsinger, a VP at Manulife responsible for the existence of the orphan policies for this company:

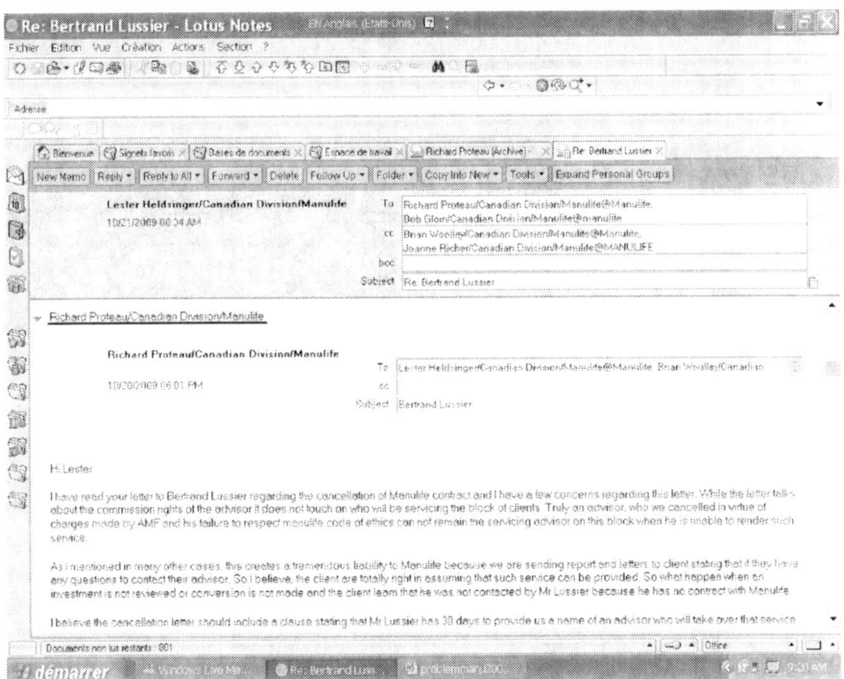

Re: Bertrand Lussier - Lotus Notes

Lester Heldsinger/Canadian Division/Manulife
10/21/2009 08:34 AM

To: Richard Proteau/Canadian Division/Manulife@Manulife, Bob Gloin/Canadian Division/Manulife@manulife
cc: Brian Woolley/Canadian Division/Manulife@Manulife, Joanne Richer/Canadian Division/Manulife@MANULIFE
bcc:
Subject: Re: Bertrand Lussier

Richard Proteau/Canadian Division/Manulife

Richard Proteau/Canadian Division/Manulife
10/20/2009 06:01 PM

To: Lester Heldsinger/Canadian Division/Manulife@Manulife, Brian Woolley/Canadian
cc:
Subject: Bertrand Lussier

Hi Lester

I have read your letter to Bertrand Lussier regarding the cancellation of Manulife contract and I have a few concerns regarding this letter. While the letter talks about the commission rights of the advisor it does not touch on who will be servicing the block of clients. Truly an advisor, who we cancelled in virtue of charges made by AMF and his failure to respect manulife code of ethics can not remain the servicing advisor on this block when he is unable to render such service.

As I mentioned in many other cases, this creates a tremendous liability to Manulife because we are sending report and letters to client stating that if they have any questions to contact their advisor. So I believe, the client are totally right in assuming that such service can be provided. So what happen when an investment is not reviewed or conversion is not made and the client learn that he was not contacted by Mr Lussier because he has no contract with Manulife.

I believe the cancellation letter should include a clause stating that Mr Lussier has 30 days to provide us a name of an advisor who will take over that service

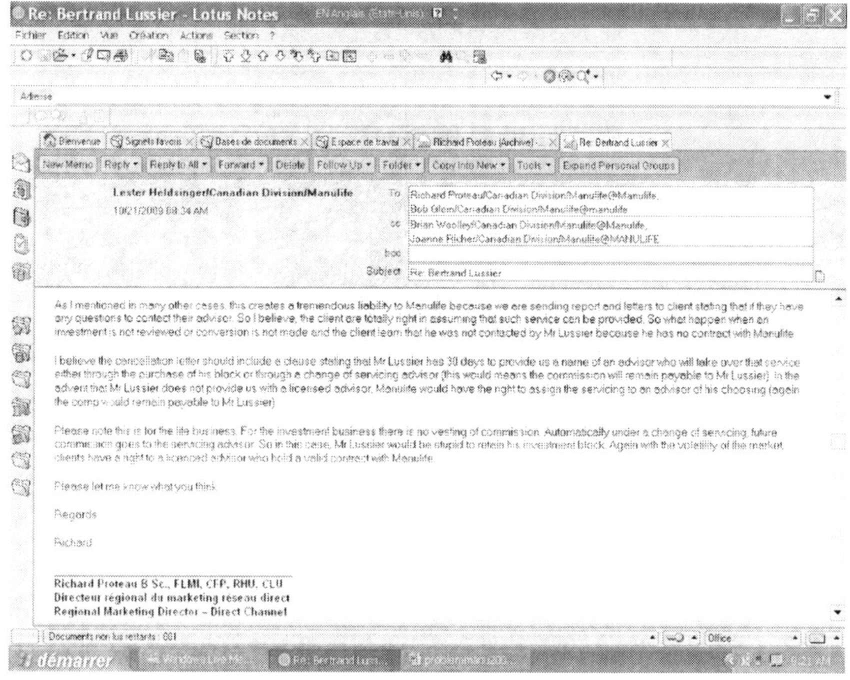

Re: Bertrand Lussier - Lotus Notes

Lester Heldsinger/Canadian Division/Manulife
10/21/2009 08:34 AM

To: Richard Proteau/Canadian Division/Manulife@Manulife, Bob Glem/Canadian Division/Manulife@manulife
cc: Brian Woolley/Canadian Division/Manulife@Manulife, Joanne Richer/Canadian Division/Manulife@MANULIFE
bcc:
Subject: Re: Bertrand Lussier

As I mentioned in many other cases, this creates a tremendous liability to Manulife because we are sending report and letters to client stating that if they have any questions to contact their advisor. So I believe, the client are totally right in assuming that such service can be provided. So what happen when an investment is not reviewed or conversion is not made and the client learn that he was not contacted by Mr Lussier because he has no contract with Manulife

I believe the cancellation letter should include a clause stating that Mr Lussier has 30 days to provide us a name of an advisor who will take over that service either through the purchase of his block or through a change of servicing advisor (this would means the commission will remain payable to Mr Lussier). In the advent that Mr Lussier does not provide us with a licensed advisor, Manulife would have the right to assign the servicing to an advisor of his choosing (again the comp would remain payable to Mr Lussier)

Please note this is for the life business. For the investment business there is no vesting of commission. Automatically under a change of servicing, future commission goes to the servicing advisor. So in this case, Mr Lussier would be stupid to retain his investment block. Again with the volatility of the market clients have a right to a licensed advisor who hold a valid contract with Manulife.

Please let me know what you think.

Regards

Richard

Richard Proteau B Sc., FLMI, CFP, RHU, CLU
Directeur régional du marketing réseau direct
Regional Marketing Director – Direct Channel

There is a last kind of orphan policies. Those resulting from the perpetration of a criminal act.

When I was with Manulife, I witnessed the destruction of lapse notices for old life policies. The insurer had no valid address of the policy owner because the name of the agent had been removed (replaced by the term "default"). The address of the policy owner was not kept up to date because there was no agent looking after the policy. As a result, the policy owners never received their lapse notices and the notices were simply destroyed. Here is the proof in one of these lapse notices I was able to save from destruction:

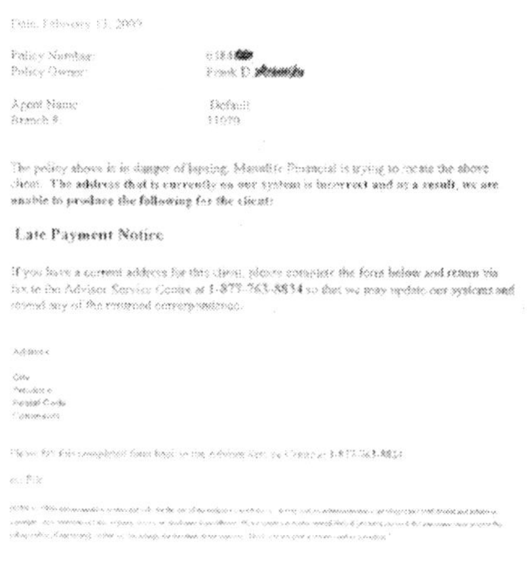

LAPSE WARNING

Policy Number:
Policy Owner: Frank D.

Agent Name: Default
Branch #: 11070

The policy above is in danger of lapsing. Manulife Financial is trying to locate the above client. The address that is currently on our system is incorrect and as a result, we are unable to produce the following for the client:

Late Payment Notice

If you have a current address for this client, please complete the form below and return via fax to the Advisor Service Centre at 1-877-763-8834 so that we may update our systems and resend any of the returned correspondence.

Address

City
Province
Postal Code

The undeniable proven fact is that orphan clients have a higher lapse rate. This lapse rate increases the insurer's profit since the clients do not take advantage of their insurance options that could cost insurers a lot of money. The insurer won't have to pay the death benefit and can cash in on the release of the reserves associated with these policies. As we shall see in the next chapter, when you link the orphan policies to toxic policies, the achieved lapse rate will determine whether the insurer incurs an astronomical loss or makes an astronomical profit.

Finally, for clients who still have a servicing advisor on their Universal Life, this servicing advisor is denied the tool necessary to manage the risk of your Universal Life. This tool is an inforce illustration software that would allow the advisor to do new projections against what was illustrated. Only one company made certain that for each product released there was an inforce illustration software and this company was Maritime Life. Sadly, the high standards of Maritime Life disappeared with its acquisition by Manulife.

All advisors must order inforce illustrations from an insurer's Head Office, usually staffed by a few overworked employees that cannot run many simulations. This is why policy holders of Universal Life rarely see an inforce illustration. This practice is criminal considering how complex a Universal Life is and how many variables can change the expected cash values.

Rule#14: Request a service commitment in writing from the advisor you are purchasing this product through , and even include the caveat that the commission must be repaid if the advisor breaches this service contract.

(10) http://www.hatton.ca

ORPHAN POLICES AND TOXIC POLICIES

"Insurers, in their pricing of Universal Life, made the bet that consumers would be stupid enough to surrender their policy not understanding they had prepaid their insurance allowing the insurer to put the amount of the prepayment in their corporate pockets." (Richard Proteau)

What are lapse supported policies?

Lapse supported insurance policies are life insurance products that have a level cost of insurance where the insurer in determining the cost of insurance have made an assumption that a certain number of policy owners will surrender their policies. By assuming there will be less claims paid on death because a certain number of policy owners have cancelled their policies, the insurer can reduce the cost of insurance it will charge under this product. The insurer will also assume that policy owners will surrender their policies in the early years forfeiting the insurance they have prepaid which is taken as profits by the insurer.

Pricing based on lapse support is like a thin razor wire that insurers must walk upon. If too many policies lapse, there will not be enough policy owners paying premiums to pay future claims. If not enough policies lapse, too many claims will have to be paid for the premium that have been collected.

What are toxic policies?

The pricing on insurance policies with level cost of insurance is based on two main assumptions. It is based on lapse rates and interest rates.

Unprofitable life policies are insurance products where the pricing is inadequate to pay for the amount of future claims that the insurer will incur. This is because the insurer will be unable to meet one of the assumptions made in the pricing of the product. As a result, the insurer will be responsible to allocate its own reserves to deal with this profit gap. While unprofitable, the insurer still has options available to rectify the profitability of these policies.

Toxic policies are the equivalent of the perfect pricing storm whereby two assumptions used in the pricing of the policy come together to make the product so unprofitable that there is only one option available for the insurer in dealing with these policies. These policies must lapse! These policies must be taken off their balance sheet and this mean that the policy owners must act against their best interest and surrender these policies.

The two assumptions used in the pricing that have created this perfect pricing storm are lapse rates and interest rates. Low interest rates have significantly increased the cost of insurance of new Universal Life. For Universal Life where the insurer used an 8% interest rate in the pricing in the past, it already had a cost of insurance that was tremendously low. This gap between past and new cost of insurance of Universal Life, fueled by current low interest rates, is costing insurers a lot of money. In addition, there is now such a difference between the cost of insurance of old policies versus new policies, that policy owners have become aware of this and they have decided to hold on to these policies. This destroys the lapse assumption made in the pricing of the policies increasing further the losses of the insurer to such a level that this makes these policies toxic to the insurer. This was confirmed by Superintendant Julie Dickson, Office of Superintendant of Financial Institutions Canada:

"I have attended this conference on several occasions in the past and one that I remember particularly well was in November 2005. There was a session on the history of toxic products in Canada. A reinsurer provided all the gory details. He said that the first major Canadian insurance industry toxic product was "Term to 100", offered in the 1980s. This product was a great idea at the time, but the problem was that early years' premiums far exceeded expected claims, and later years premiums were far less than claims.

The industry had assumed that lapses would be the same as with other products, and they were not – the educated guesses turned out to be horribly wrong and the consumer response was more sophisticated than expected." (11)

The conspiracy to increase lapses on toxic life insurance policies

Since people did not want to surrender their now very valuable insurance policies, some insurers had to devise a stratagem to increase lapses. The perfect solution was to deny service and information to the policy owners by orphaning them. It is well proven that orphan policies where the policy owners do not have access to a licensed advisor have a higher lapse rate. However for some companies such as Manulife the passive creation of orphan policies was not enough. A more direct approach was required and I was a witness to this approach.

Under oath, I can state that Manulife took the name of advisors off certain block of policies. I can also state that these orphan policies were then hidden under inexistent insurance branches. I can swear since I witnessed it that changes of address were not done on these policies because no advisor was responsible for these policies. As a result, lapse notices were not sent to policy owners to inform them that their policies were about to lapse. These lapse notices were instead simply destroyed. I was a witness of this and I have proof as per the lapse notice I was able to save shown in the previous chapter. In average, I witnessed the destruction of 5 to 10 lapse notices per week which amounts at a minimum to $500,000 to $1 million of death benefit per week which the insurer will not have to pay in the future.

I called this a conspiracy because I have tried to contact all of the regulators to inform them of the criminal actions of Manulife. Not one regulator returned my call, interviewed me or accepted to look at the proof in my possession. This is not surprising because it is clear that regulators have been aware of the existence of the orphan policies for more than 20 years and could be held jointly responsible for all the death benefit not paid to policy owners. The people involved in this conspiracy are:

Manulife

Guy Couture: Vice president at Manulife. Having done an audit of the Direct Channel of Manulife that had been under his supervision, I uncovered an astronomical number of infractions he was directly responsible for. By lying, he was able to shift the blame to others. He promoted the idea of pan-Canadian operations which ignore differences in provincial regulations particularly in Quebec. The high number of orphan policies in Quebec can be directly attributed to him. He also lied in several statements made when the existence of these orphan polices were almost made public. He is now involved in trying to influence advisors in Quebec to not act according to their code of ethics by making threats to cancel their contract if they reveal to the policy owner he could enter into a life settlement to get a settlement much higher than the cash surrender value of the policy.

Lester Heldsinger: Vice president at Manulife, he continued what Guy Couture started. He is known to have lied in a letter that he sent to 500 policy owners in regards to their orphan status. He is also known to continuously have allowed advisors suspended by the regulator to continue representing themselves as servicing agent.

Brian Woolley: Working under Heldsinger, he lied in several investigations such as the investigation of Deguire's infractions. When informed of the existence of the orphan policies where the name of the advisor had disappeared, he shrugged it off and then later lied in regards to statements made by Manulife when one advisor sued Manulife.

Bureau Decision et Revision

To stop Manulife from committing infractions in Quebec, I requested an injunction from this administrative tribunal to stop Manulife operations in Quebec. This administrative tribunal in charge of the protection of the public in the financial industry refused to act under the guise that it did not have the competency to do so leading to the conclusion that Manulife was too big for the law. The judges are:

Alain Gelinas
Claude St Pierre
Leonard Serafini

Regulators

All regulators and in particular the Autorite Marche Financier (AMF) have refused to see me or hear my testimony. They also have refused to view the proofs in my possession. Their strategy was simple "hear no evil and see no evil". The employees involved are:

Yan Paquette: Director at the AMF. To protect Manulife, Yan Paquette as confirmed by Marie Pettigrew, made several proofs of Manulife wrongdoings disappear. He tried to give credibility to Manulife lies by using his power to start a campaign of defamation against me. He broke the law and committed a criminal infraction under the Quebec criminal code by helping Manulife in its retaliations against me when I became a whistleblower against this company. He now works as an advisor for the Department of Justice.

Marie Pettigrew: Director at the AMF, she started the defamation campaign against me when by letter I informed her that I held the AMF directly responsible for the existence of the orphan policies as a result of their willingness to look the other way while Manulife was breaking the law. Her defamation attempts were pathetic trying to hold me responsible for Manulife activities at a time when I was not even working for Manulife

Helene Barabe: Under the pretext of an interview with me where she refused to look at the proofs pertaining to orphan policies, she tried to impose confidentiality and therefore silence on the pretext of a fictitious investigation all done in order to stop me from talking publicly about orphan policies.

Superior court of Quebec

In trying to get justice for myself and thousands of orphan policy owners, I sued the AMF for defamation. The goal was to subpoena Yan Paquette and Marie Pettigrew to interrogate them on their actions. Three judges literally conspired to stop me from questioning Yan Paquette and Marie Pettigrew on anything associated with orphan policies in order to protect the AMF and Manulife from criminal accusations and accusations of fraud. Two of these judges are:

Judge Francoeur: This judge conspired with the AMF to censor all of the information regarding Manulife criminal activities. He wrote a decision to prevent the interrogation of Yan Paquette and Marie Pettigrew which would have implicated the AMF in this fraud.

Judge April: She made certain that the plan of judge Francoeur came to fruition.

It is important to note that because of these 2 judges, thousands of policy owners have been prevented from learning that they had illegitimately lost their insurance policies following the criminal actions from Manulife.

Jean-Francois Michaud of Ogilvy Renault: This lawyer who represented Manulife knowingly included lies or statements he ought to have known as lies in his response to a civil lawsuit against Manulife to hide the criminal actions of Manulife in regards to the orphan policies where the name of the advisors had been removed. , He left his firm to become a judge for the Court of Quebec.

(11) http://www.osfi-bsif.gc.ca/Eng/Docs/jd20101108.pdf

MAKING A COMPLAINT AGAINST YOUR ADVISOR

"Don't follow any advice an advisor is giving until he has proven he can be trusted." (Richard Proteau)

Your advisor presented and sold to you a fraudulent Universal Life illustration with the help of the insurer and now you are realizing that Universal Life is a lousy investment. One that will cost you a lot of money. You are ready to make a complaint against your advisor. Though this is what you want to do, it is not the correct action to take at this point.. You would be skipping many steps and this could prevent you from getting your money back.

First it must be determined whether this situation is the result of an error or an omission on the advisor's part. Do not skip this step. Too often clients forget that their advisor is insured against errors and omissions. By making an official complaint with a regulator and claiming either fraud or gross negligence, you would be jeopardizing your opportunity to be compensated under the error and omission insurance of the advisor.

It is important to deal with the advisor before involving the regulator. First, try to determine what was the driving factor that negatively impacted your Universal Life values versus the illustrated values. Then send a registered letter to the advisor asking him to explain the difference in the results. If the advisor made an error, do not escalate further until you know whether you can be compensated under such a claim.

For example, if the advisor illustrated at 6% without knowing that this was net of MER (you would be surprised how many advisors don't know this as insurers don't educate advisors on this fact) and the real rate of illustration was close to 10%, this is not fraud or negligence on his part. He did not know and could not have known since the insurers keeps this as their little secret. This is an error as far as I am concerned. A claim should be made against the advisor under his error and omission insurance. You don't lose anything in making this claim but you can lose everything in not making it. Let the insurer of the error and omission insurance go after the insurer that did not train its agent sufficiently in the use of its software in order to recover the money it has paid to you in the settlement of your claim.

If you are not successful in dealing with this as an error, you can then escalate to the regulator. Remember though, you have to be careful because regulators are not there to protect you (we will discuss this further in another chapter). Escalating a problem to the regulator can provide you with the satisfaction that the advisor will be sanctioned , but it will not help you in any way recover the money you have lost. In fact, any fine that the advisor has to pay out to the regulator could actually reduce his ability to compensate you for your losses. None of the fine paid to a regulator is ever used to compensate victims. Fraud and infractions represent good business for the government.

If you want to recover your money, you will have to do it on your own through an individual lawsuit or as part of a group under a class action.

Rule #15 Simplicity beats complex advice every time!

DEALING WITH THE INSURER

"Insurers have demonstrated repeatedly that they are not big enough to admit their mistakes, smart enough to learn from them, and ethical enough not to repeat them." (Richard Proteau)

If you believe the insurer is responsible for your Universal Life policy performing poorly, compared to what had been projected on the illustration, then you are entirely right. The insurer is responsible, but don't expect them to admit it.

They will deal with your complaints using standard objections and, if you are not prepared, you may fall into the trap of believing them. These are the 2 objections they will try to use:

1. Advisors are independent and therefore they, the insurer, are not responsible for the advice given to you by the independent advisor.

2. You have signed a disclaimer stating that you understood the returns were not guaranteed.

We already have discussed the disclaimer page. As for the advisor being independent, this does not in any way change the fact that insurers are responsible for the tools they provide to advisors. If their tool is faulty or if the insurance companies do not provide the training required in the correct use these sales and marketing tools,

they are then liable for the advice that resulted from the misuse of these tools.

There are already several judgments that support this argument in Quebec. These judgments are:

1. Ward versus Manulife

"Claim goes on to state that, "Manufacturers provided the plaintiff with computer generated illustrations which promoted the sale of a policy. The illustrations were developed at Manufacturers' home office as part of an overall scheme to mislead customers into believing that their whole life "vanishing premiums" policies had attributes which in fact such policies did not possess. The illustrations, along with an orchestrated set of sales techniques, misrepresented the terms, benefits and advantages of the Manufacturers' policies in order to include the plaintiff and other members of the plaintiff class to purchase such policies."

[137] No action was commenced against sales representatives, brokers or agents and, of course, the claims arose out of policies sold by many Manulife agents.

[138] In paragraph 8, it is alleged that "Manufacturers' agents attended training sessions and/or were provided with sales manuals, all of which were designed to encourage Manufacturers' agents to rely upon the computer-generated illustrations to sell the "vanishing premium" policies. The agents were not informed of the real risks and costs inherent in the "vanishing premium" policies. Manufacturers' agents were provided with software and/or sample illustrations which allowed them to demonstrate the manner in which the policies operated to potential policy holders."

[139] In paragraph 9, it is alleged that, "Manufacturers' representations with respect to these policies were false. Manufacturers' dividends scales, interest rate and investment return projections, and result in policy and dividend illustrations were inconsistent with or contrary to Manufacturers' internal forecast, estimates, analysis or projections concerning future interest rates and dividends."

[140] In paragraph 10, it is alleged that Manufacturers' "knew or ought to have known that the policy would not perform as forecasted..." and that "it would be necessary for the plaintiff to make further premium payments, and that the obligation to pay premiums would not "vanish" as promised or at all."

[141] In paragraph 11, it is alleged that "Manufacturers' omitted from its illustrations and sales materials and concealed from its agents, and its customers, including the plaintiff and the class of plaintiffs, material facts regarding the Manufacturers' illustrations and the performance of these policies, including such facts as the extreme volatility of the products as illustrated, the highly interest-sensitive nature of the illustrations used to induce sales of such products, and the substantial effect of even minor variations in interest rates on the performance illustrated." I observe that, because this class action was settled without any admission of liability, Manulife's culpability was never adjudicated upon."

NOTE: Replace "sensitive and volatile nature of interest rates" by 'volatility of returns linked to market indices" and you would get exactly the same stratagem employed by the Vanishing Premium and therefore resulting in the same judgment as reached in Ward versus Manulife.

2. Lafreniere versus Transamerica

3. Latreille versus Industrial

DISCRIMINATION: THE LAST LEVEL OF DECEPTION

"Discrimination is the better part of underwriting. It should never become the better part of deception.." (Richard Proteau)

Imagine that a deaf person goes to eat at a restaurant. The restaurant has the policy of automatically applying a 15% service charge to the bill. At the end of the meal, this customer gets his bill and in reviewing it, he is surprised to see that the service charge has been increased to 30%. When the deaf patron asks why, the reply to him is that deaf people like him require more work to serve and therefore they should be charged more.

Do we believe for one moment this restaurant would not be facing discrimination charges?

Why is the insurance industry doing the same?

What I am about to describe is the most vile, dishonest, repugnant, and unprofessional practice in the insurance industry that I had witnessed in my entire career. Sadly, I am the sole person in the insurance industry who had the courage to publicly condemn this practice. What is this practice? Discrimination outside of underwriting

Underwriting is all about discrimination. It is about determining the state of the insured's health and charging a premium based upon that state of health. Unhealthy people are discriminated against, but this is considered legal because it is the nature of individual insurance to charge a premium in relation to the risk you represent.

Let's look at this example. The client, HadCancer , has been cancer free for 5 years and he would like to see if he could get some life insurance. He contacts an agent who completes a life insurance application on his behalf which he then submits to Insurer A. The premium is $5,000 for $250,000 of Universal Life. Unlike other advisors, Advisor A. discloses his commission to HadCancer by giving him the commission page produced by the illustration software. The commission page shows that Advisor A. will make $3,000 in base commission, if the policy is issued and taken.

This is the first problem. The commission disclosure is incomplete. It does not include the investment bonus of 150% the advisor will also receive (an additional $4,500).

The application goes through underwriting and Advisor A. is informed that the company can insure HadCancer, but there will be a permanent rating applied to the policy. This permanent rating is 100% and means that the minimum premium of the Universal Life increases, doubling to $10,000.

After talking to Advisor A., client HadCancer is convinced that this is still a good offer and he accepts it. Two years after the policy is issued, he learns from another advisor that he could reduce the permanent rating from 100% down to 50%, and possibly even remove it, by dealing with Insurer B. How is this possible?

HadCancer would probably be very surprised to learn that Insurer A had doubled the commission to Advisor A, to a total of $15,000 including the investment bonus (twice the original amount of commission and bonus), if Advisor A. convinced the client to accept the policy with the rated offer of 100%. This increase in commission was not disclosed to the client.

In addition, this sale increased Advisor A.'s total sales and as a result his bonus level increased to 160%; a 10% increase which will be paid on all business he submitted through the year. This increase is worth another $5,000 to Advisor A. By convincing HadCancer to accept the rating that underwriters for Insurer A had determined, Advisor A. made a total of $20,000 in commission plus bonus, versus the original $7,500 (of which 3,000 $ only had been disclosed). Why would Advisor A. work harder and get a better rating for his client when it benefits him to get paid so much for doing less?

When advisors are asked why they should receive more commission on cases involving clients that have a medical condition resulting in a permanent rating, they will all state that it's because the rated clients represent a lot more work in order to convince them to take the offered policies. I disagree. Insureds with medical conditions want and need the insurance even more than healthier clients and therefore take less convincing to take the policy offered. Based upon this bit of reality the advisor should be paid less, in my opinion.

The practice that we have witnessed through the above example is morally wrong. It is deception based upon discrimination. It is a conflict of interest and we cannot state that an advisor will remain objective to the client's needs when he will get paid $20,000 versus $7,500, for convincing a client to take a less than favorable rating.

Remember as well that the increase in commission due to the permanent rating is never disclosed to the clients. Once again, this is wrong.

THE LAW

At its best, insurance is the noblest of financial products; separated from law and ethics it is the worst. (an adaptation of an Aristotle quote)

There are many existing laws that should prevent the actuaries of insurance companies from designing software that would produce fraudulent illustrations. It is against the law to advertise false prices for a product or service. Why is this practice accepted in the insurance industry? Is it because nobody complains?

The fact is, many people saw the fraud of false illustrations coming and tried to prevent it. Such a person is William Podmore, who went on a crusade to protect the rights of policy holders. When he gave his opinion in regards to Bill C-8, an act to establish the Financial Consumer Agency, he stated this before the Parliament of Canada:

"As our fourth concern, we also concur with the comments by Senator Leo Kolber, as reported in the Financial Post of Thursday, June 22, 2000, that the vision of this bill is inadequate and that it fails to set out a broad vision or blueprint for the unfolding financial services industry.

As we see it, the proposed legislation does not adequately address the issues of full, plain, and adequate disclosure to consumers; fair, reasonable, and non-abusive transaction practices; and adequate redress mechanisms to resolve disputes.

This was discussed in task force recommendation 53."

In this we see that the provincial and federal governments knew about the fraudulent representations made by insurers in regards to selling Universal Life. The governments chose to protect the insurers instead of consumers. They chose to not apply the laws, such as provincial laws like the ONTARIO REGULATION 7/00 UNFAIR OR DECEPTIVE ACTS OR PRACTICES:

"1. For the purposes of the definition of "unfair or deceptive act or practice" in section 438 of the Act, each of the following actions is prescribed as an unfair or deceptive act or practice:

4. Any illustration, circular, memorandum or statement that misrepresents, or by omission is so incomplete that it misrepresents, terms, benefits or advantages of any policy or contract of insurance issued or to be issued."

Illustrations for Universal Life are illegal under federal law, such as:

74.01 (1) A person engages in reviewable conduct who, for the purpose of promoting, directly or indirectly, the supply or use of a product or for the purpose of promoting, directly or indirectly, any business interest, by any means whatever,

(a) makes a representation to the public that is false or misleading in a material respect;

(b) makes a representation to the public in the form of a statement, warranty or guarantee of the performance, efficacy or length of life of a product that is not based on an adequate and proper test thereof, the proof of which lies on the person making the representation; or

(c) makes a representation to the public in a form that purports to be

(i) a warranty or guarantee of a product, or

(ii) a promise to replace, maintain or repair an article or any part thereof or to repeat or continue a service until it has achieved a specified result,

if the form of purported warranty or guarantee or promise is materially misleading or if there is no reasonable prospect that it will be carried out.

When the federal or provincial governments are contacted in regards to the illustrations of insurers that constitute infractions of these laws, the government refuses to intervene and instead refers the issue back to the insurers. This is akin to police referring victims back to the criminals. Who is regulating the insurance industry? The government or the insurers? Here is the answer of the federal government:

Competition Bureau / Bureau de la concurrence
To Richard_proteau@yahoo.com
CC compbureau@cb-bc.gc.ca Jul 17, 2013
Our File: R625821

Dear Mr. Proteau:

Thank you for the information you provided to the Competition Bureau regarding Canadian Life and Health Insurance Association.

The role of the Bureau, as an independent law enforcement agency, is to ensure that Canadian businesses and consumers prosper in a competitive and innovative marketplace. Information brought to our attention by consumers and businesses is very important to our work as it contributes to the identification of marketplace issues. The Bureau takes all allegations of false or misleading representations and deceptive marketing practices seriously.

Due to the large number of complaints we receive, we have established criteria for the selection of cases to ensure that our decision to pursue or not pursue a particular case is exercised in an objective and consistent manner. We consider, for example, factors such as the scope of the conduct, the number of consumers and/or businesses adversely affected, the financial loss caused by the practice, the number of complaints received and the available evidence.

The information you have provided will be recorded and entered into our database and it may be used to develop or support future enforcement activities under the laws we enforce. As a law enforcement agency, the Bureau is required to conduct its investigations in private. As such, we cannot provide complaint status

reports or comment further on this matter in order to protect the integrity of the investigative process.

We invite you to visit our Web site, www.competitionbureau.gc.ca, to learn more about the work of the Bureau and to access public information on case developments and general information about our programs and activities.

Thank you again for taking the time to bring this matter to our attention.

Tomek Cygalski
Agent de la mise en application | Direction générale des pratiques loyales des affaires Enforcement Support Officer | Fair Business Practices Branch
1-800-348-5358 | télécopieur / facsimile 819-997-0324 | ATS/TTY 1-800-642-3844

There is no better proof of a regulator protecting insurers than a statement from the Ontario regulator that refers concerns back to the offending parties.

"On July 14, 2013, you sent me an e-mail pertaining to the use of constant interest rates in Life Insurance Illustrations and how these affect the future values of universal policies. You feel this constitutes an Unfair and Deceptive Act or Practice under Ontario Regulation 07/00. Based on the evidence you have provided, we cannot conclude that these parameters are in and of themselves unfair or deceptive, as each case must be considered on its own merits. You asked for a disclaimer to be added to these illustrations. You may wish to raise your concerns with the CLHIA. Bien à vous, Manon Azar Compliance Officer FSCO"

And more examples of this conspiracy of silence:

Godin, Ronald (CAI-DMA)
To me Jul 15, 2013

Your complaint has been referred directly to the Office of the Superintendant of Insurance for NB.

Ronald Godin
Consumer Advocate for Insurance
Défenseur du consommateur en matière d'assurances
From: Richard Proteau [mailto:richard_proteau@yahoo.com]
Sent: 14 juillet 2013 3:13
To: Godin, Ronald (CAI-DMA)
Subject: Re: orphan policies

Hi Mr. Godin,

I aknowledge your message. Please note I have studied carefully the Consumer Advocate Act.

Section 9(3) If the Consumer Advocate refuses to investigate or ceases to investigate any complaint, the Consumer Advocate shall advise the complainant and provide reasons for the decision to do so.

Sadly while you explain that this does not fall within your mandate you do not provide any reasons.

To be specific since I do not believe my complaint is frivolous, the only reason left is that after studying what I have sent you have determined that my complaints was about violations of the Insurance Act and therefore under :

9(9) Notwithstanding subsection (7), where during the course of an investigation the Consumer Advocate reasonably believes the insurer, broker or agent has violated any prohibition or failed to comply with the requirements of the Insurance Act, the Consumer Advocate shall
(a) suspend the investigation and refer the matter to the Superintendent, or (b) complete the investigation and communicate to the Superintendent the results of the investigation and any recommendations, including any opinion and the reasons for the recommendations.

Has my complaint being referred under section 9(9)

thank you for confirming

Regards

Richard Proteau
From: "Godin, Ronald (CAI-DMA)" <ronald.godin@gnb.ca>
To:"'Richard_proteau@yahoo.com'" <Richard_proteau@yahoo.com>
Cc: "Godin, Sandra (CAI-DMA)" <Sandra.Godin@gnb.ca>; "Ramsay, Anne-Marie (CAI-DMA)" <Anne-Marie.Ramsay@gnb.ca>
Sent: Thursday, July 11, 2013 2:49:07 PM
Subject: FW: orphan policies

Mr. Proteau....I have forwarded your email messages to Mr. David Weir, Deputy Superintendant of Insurance for the Province of NB. This matter is not within our mandate but rather within the mandate of the office in question or the new Financial and Consumer Services Commission of NB.

Ronald Godin
Consumer Advocate for Insurance
Défenseur du consommateur en matière d'assurances
From: Lafortune, Pauline (CAI-DMA)
Sent: 2 juillet 2013 11:58
To: Godin, Sandra (CAI-DMA); Godin, Ronald (CAI-DMA); Ramsay, Anne-Marie (CAI-DMA)
Subject: FW: orphan policies

New file!

Pauline Lafortune
Administrative Assistant/ Adjointe Administrative
Office of the Consumer Advocate for Insurance
Bureau du défenseur du consommateur en matière d'assurances
Tel: 506-549-5560 or/ ou 1-888-283-5111

From: Richard Proteau [mailto:richard_proteau@yahoo.com]
Sent: 1 juillet 2013 21:10
To: Lafortune, Pauline (CAI-DMA)
Subject: orphan policies

Dear Consumer Advocate for Insurance,

You will find attach a press release in regards to a recent Notice published by the Autorite des Marches Financiers advising insurers and advisors that the existence of orphan policies in the insurance industry of this province is a violation of several laws in this province.

I have reviewed the Insurance Act of New Brunswick, and my conclusion is that the same violations are occurring in New Brunswick. Below you will find the statutes of the Insurance Act about the subject matter.

Please note that I have proofs, having in my possession faxed lapse notices from Manulife that the existence of the orphan policies constitutes an inducement to lapse and surrender of policies. The fact that policyowners of orphan policies receive annual reports telling them to contact unlicensed agents for information creates the idea with these customers that a licensed agent is taking care of their policy when this is not the case. It promotes lapses and target old age policy owners who are not mentally apt to manage their policies.

I am available for any questions you may have.

Richard Proteau (902-931-0097)

Statutes of the Insurance Act in question:

351No person shall act or offer or undertake to act or represent himself as an insurance agent, broker, adjuster or damage appraiser in this Province unless he holds a subsisting licence issued under this Act or is otherwise authorized to do so under this Act.

362Any person who not being duly licensed as an agent, broker, adjuster or damage appraiser represents or holds himself out to the public as being such an agent, broker, adjuster or damage appraiser or as being engaged in the insurance business, by means of advertisements, cards, circulars, letterheads, signs or other methods or, being duly licensed as such agent, broker, adjuster or damage appraiser advertises as aforesaid or carries on such business in any other name than that stated in the licence is guilty of an offence.

1968, c.6, s.359; 1976, c.34, s.10.

368(1)No insurer licensed under this Act, and no officer, agent or employee of such an insurer, and no insurance agent or broker authorized under this Act, shall directly or indirectly, pay or allow, or offer or agree to pay or allow, any commission or other compensation or anything of value to any person for acting or attempting or assuming to act as an insurance agent or broker in respect of insurance in the Province or for having or claiming or appearing to have any influence or control over the insured or prospect for insurance unless that person holds at the time a subsisting insurance agent's or broker's licence or is a person acting under the authority of subsection 352(15), (16), (17) or (18).

369(1)Any person licensed as an agent for life insurance under this Act who induces, directly or indirectly, an insured to lapse, forfeit or surrender for cash, or for paid up or extended insurance, or for other valuable consideration, his contract of life insurance with one insurer in order to effect a contract of life insurance with another insurer, or makes any false or misleading statement or representation in the solicitation or negotiation of insurance, or coerces or proposes, directly or indirectly, to coerce a prospective buyer of life insurance through the influence of a business or a professional relationship or otherwise, to give a preference in respect to the placing of life insurance which would not be otherwise given in the effecting of a life insurance contract, is guilty of an offence.

369.2No person shall engage in any unfair or deceptive act or practice in the business of insurance.

1980, c.27, s.9.

No compensation except to licensee

39 (1) No insurer, and no licensed agent shall, directly or indirectly, pay, or allow, or offer or agree to pay or allow, any commission or other compensation or anything of value to any person in respect of the effecting or negotiating or placing of any contract or renewal thereof unless that person holds a license that is in force under this Part.

Inducing policyholder to lapse or surrender

43 No person shall, by means of a false or misleading representation, procure or induce, or attempt to procure or induce any person to forfeit, lapse or surrender a policy. R.S., c. 231, s. 43.

Press Release: Precisions on the Notice of the AMF regarding orphan policies ttp://www.lautorite.qc.ca/files/pdf/bulletin/2013/vol10no20/vol10no20_3-1.pdf

On may 23rd, the l'Autorité des Marchés Financiers (AMF) announce in the Notice above (in French only) that the existence of orphan policies constituted infractions under article 16 of the Act respecting the distribution of financial products and services, L.R.Q., c. D-9.2, and also under articles 4, 23 and 24 of the code of ethics of the la Chambre Financiere R.R.Q., c. D-9.2, r. 3.and under article 222.2 of the Insurance Act L.R.Q., c. A-32.

I am publishing this press release in the interest of the truth. The notice in question gives the impression that only the advisors and insurance companies are responsible for this very serious situation. The truth is that the AMF knew of the existence of the infractions represented by orphan policies for more than 20 years but decided to turn a blind eye to this situation and to not apply the law.

It has now been almost 3 year since I approached the AMF with proofs regarding the existence of orphan policies in the Direct Channel of Manulife with these proofs demonstrating that clients were losing their insurance coverage because of the orphan status of their policies. I asked the intervention of the AMF to protect anymore orphan clients from losing their insurance. The reaction of the AMF was akin to a spoiled child who does not want to recognize the truth by crying, shouting, hitting and jumping up and down. This was the reaction of the AMF when confronted with the information I had. The AMF went as far as to attack the messenger in the hope that the truth would disappear

But I remained firm in my belief that the existence of orphan policies was illegal and did not waver in maintaining this position even in the face of this irrational behavior of the AMF explaining to its lawyers that not applying the law created an unacceptable situation. When the AMF still refused to listen to me, I decided to use a heavy hand with this organization to make myself understood. When the law is applied on a discriminatory basis, it is a violation of the Charter of Rights and Freedoms and there has to be consequences. As a result, I have introduced a request for a declaratory judgment 200-17-017919-135 in the Superior Court of Quebec to render certain articles of the Act pertaining to the distribution of financial products and services unconstitutional. This request will be heard on June 17th and 18th where a judge will decide if this request is receivable with Stein Monast representing the AMF and Me Jennifer Tremblay, representing the Government du Québec.

It seems that the heavy hand I used has put some sense into AMF who has finally understood its obligation and responsibilities to apply the Law. The AMF has finally informed the insurance companies through this Notice that they were required to address the problem of orphan policies immediately. However it saddens me to see that the AMF is not mature enough to act rationally by gathering and analysing all of the information regarding this issue even if it means talking to me before publishing a Notice which is erroneous. I have studied the problem of the orphan policies for 5 years and I am the only expert who understands this problem.

In this Notice, the AMF falls back on its usual strategy of blaming everything on the advisors. These advisors have nothing to do with the creation of the environment leading to the problem of orphan policies which are the result of demutualisation, industry consolidation and privatization of the distribution. Many of the policies are orphaned because the advisor who sold the policy died or the corporation or firm ceased to exist. According to this notice, the dead advisor will have to reach us beyond the grave to name their replacements. Also the AMF ignores the dynamics around distribution. Many advisors selling life insurance are attached to a firm and the policies are owned by the firm and as a result it is impossible for the advisor to name his replacement on business he does not own when they exit the insurance industry.

Now that I have extracted this Notice from the AMF, is my work done? Absolutely not! First there has been a lot of victims the result of this illegal practice. These victims have lost their insurance or other rights because their policies were orphaned. These victims have the right to be compensated for their losses by those who are responsible for these damages and those who have ignored this situation such as the insurance companies, the AMF and Chambre Financiere. My next goal will be to ensure that such compensation becomes a reality.

Second, the problem of the orphan policies is not a problem unique to Quebec even if this problem is more defined in Quebec because of the existence of the Act respecting the distribution of the financial products and services; an Act which does not exist in the other provinces. Still the existence of these policies is illegal under the Insurance Act of these provinces and I sincerely hope that the regulators of the other provinces will demonstrate more maturity than the AMF by willingly informed insurance companies in their respective provinces of the requirement to address and fix this situation immediately. If this is not done I will have no other solutions than to introduce the same judicial procedures that I have used in Quebec.

Finally addressing the problem of the orphan policies is only the beginning. I intend to address all of the gaps in the laws pertaining to the life insurance industry which allow insurance companies to use unethical commercial practices which are not in the interest of the public. No subject will be ignored. My next battle will be on transfers out of the segregated funds and the lack of disclosure associated with these transfers. To reach my goal, I will publish the most comprehensive Insurance Industry report with more than 100 pages analysing the commercial practices existing in the insurance industry.

LaFleche, Paul T
To me
CC Murphy, Douglas H Cody, Elizabeth-Ann (FIN) Jun 5, 2013

Douglas Murphy will respond to you when he returns on june 17th or shortly thereafter.

Paul LaFleche
Deputy Minister

DEALING WITH THE REGULATOR

"The regulation of the sale of life insurance through its current form of licensing is the next step in the evolution of organized crime and it's called regulated crime." (Richard Proteau)

Beware of the regulators; they are not here to protect you or to help you. Infractions and frauds are good business for them. They collect millions in fines and not one cent of this is used to compensate the victims of fraud.

Most provinces have a fund to compensate victims of fraud in the financial services and this fund is managed by the regulator. When it comes down to insurance, the regulator will do everything in its power to rule out fraud because fraud when insurance is involved is too costly to be indemnified. Fraud involving insurance will include loss of insurability and therefore the claim will not be the money lost on the cash value but the loss on the death benefit which is several times larger than cash value.

The regulator will therefore try to reduce the infraction to gross negligence which means the regulator will still be able to collect its fine while making it impossible for you to get compensated under fraud or under error and omission (since error and omission does not cover gross negligence.)

In the case of Thibault in Quebec, this advisor took advantage of clients by selling them Universal Life they could not afford. He did this by falsifying and lying on the application in regards to the income of the client. The regulator concluded this was a gross negligence. You heard right! Intentionally reporting false income to issue an insurance policy that has no insurable interest for the purpose of getting astronomic commission and the regulator portrayed this as being gross negligence! As a result the victims were not compensated for fraud.

There are too many examples of such stories, I could write a book on this. The best example is the regulator Autorite des Marches Financiers in Quebec who accepted a payment of $400,000 in order to find an insurer named Desjardins not guilty of fraud for having falsified price comparison quotes through its distributor SFL by always putting the product of Desjardins has having the best price in their analysis even if this was not true.

Radio Canada produced a report which showed unequivocally that Desjardins and SFL had falsified the results of the price comparisons they were providing to clients. Desjardins was able to get off of the hook by paying $400,000 to the AMF while the victims were not told that Desjardins had conned them into buying their more expensive products.

This is why you should never trust the regulator.

"According to the Radio-Canada investigative report aired on Monday night in Quebec, Services Financiers Laurentienne (SFL) uses a "carrot and stick" approach with its in-house products, offering incentives such as trips and enhanced commissions to those who meet targets, and dismissal for those who do not.

SFL and its English counterpart Laurentian Financial Services are distributors for Desjardins Financial Security, which specializes in life and health insurance and savings products.

The report centers on one advisor, Léon Lemoine, who says he was handed his walking papers for failing to meet sales targets for in-house products. After about six months as an independent, Lemoine apparently contacted the CBC.

In the televised report, Lemoine said he became suspicious when every request for an insurance quote came back with a recommendation for the Desjardins product. When he challenged the recommendation, he was told he could buy his own analytical software and check for himself. He did.

He says he found that on every case he ran through the software, the Desjardins product ranked very low on the list of recommendations. With his own analytic capability, he began selecting insurance on his own, rarely selling Desjardins.

Lemoine says that it was this decision that led to his dismissal, as the Desjardins head office demanded his termination for failure to sell the in-house product."

In the investigative report of CBC we could see clearly on TV that Lemoine was telling the truth and that SFL's recommendation that Desjardins was the best was false and the recommendation and market analysis had been rigged in favor of Desjardins."(12)

Despite this indisputable proof, the AMF published the following statement that we saw earlier:

"Our investigation has not detected any fraudulent act by the firms that belong to the SFL network, nor has it identified anything indicating the firms' clients could have been injured or suffered damage. However, we have concluded that disclosure to consumers of the business relationships of SFL network member firms should be improved", said Jean St-Gelais, President and CEO of the AMF.

Under the terms of the agreement between SFL Management Inc. and the AMF, SFL Management has undertaken to improve disclosure practices for the business relationships of the SFL network's member firms. SFL will also pay the AMF $400,000, in particular to reimburse the costs of the investigation."

(12)http://www.advisor.ca/news/industry-news/radio-canada-35653

YOU AND YOUR LAWYER

"If you must believe in the law; first obtain power and money because without it, you will not obtain justice and without justice you can only obey the law without having any faith in it." (Richard Proteau)

I have reviewed numerous judgments in relation to individual civil lawsuits involving Universal Life. My conclusion is that the plaintiffs usually lose because of a lack of information and knowledge regarding the sale of life insurance. This is why I wrote this book. Lawyers know about the law but they don't know about life insurance and it is therefore difficult for them to ask the right questions in court. This is why in all of the lawsuits I have reviewed there were no questions asked in regards to the illustrations used to influence the plaintiff in buying the Universal Life. The information disclosed in this book has never been disclosed to judges to prove how Universal Life sales are based on deception.

This is not the fault of the lawyers. Lawyers rely on the expertise of experts. Sadly in reviewing the expertise provided by experts in the different lawsuits, I have found this expertise to be seriously lacking. These so called experts have never informed the plaintiffs of what I have divulgated in this book. There are two reasons for this. These experts lack the knowledge or the experts have been previously employed by different insurers and they are unwilling to condemn the practices of their previous employers.

The information I have disclosed can make a difference in the outcome of any lawsuits in regards to the sale practices of Universal Life by allowing you to prove the bad faith of the insurers. The information I have disclosed will also have an impact on the prescription date.

As a result, if you are considering a civil lawsuit, it is important to ask the lawyer if he has read this book. Before retaining the services of an expert, ask them questions about the topics discussed in this book.

The best example of the failure of a civil lawsuit because the information contained in this book was not available is Cardinal Morello c. BMO Nesbitt Burns Services financiers inc. 2013 QCCS 3991. In this trial, the expert did not question the illustration and therefore the following questions were not raised at trial:

1. The client could choose a 3% interest rate guaranteed for life. However he thought he could do better than 3%. Did he understand that to beat 3% guaranteed by investing in an index fund, he had to earn a minimum of 6% total return which would give his 3% after the MER of 3% is deducted?

2. The most conservative illustration was done at 6%. Did he understand this represented a total return of 9%? There is no way a constant 9% total return was appropriate when considering the investment selected.

3. Having failed to achieve the 9% return, the client decided to take more risk and invest into a balanced fund which was more volatile. No illustration was done to illustrate that volatility. The only point of reference for the client was the original illustration at 6%. That illustration at a constant rate of return of 6% was not valid anymore.

4. The client had selected the 'minimizer' which minimized the death benefit based on cash value. Did he understand that the death benefit minimized could not be recovered if the market rebounded?

5. An illustration of 8% was done. This represented at minimum 11.5% total return earned every year for the life of the policy. This was inappropriate! Was this done to take advantage of the conditional bonus based on 8%?

6. When the cost of insurance was changed from YRT to level COI cancelling the minimizer, was it disclosed to the client that since the policy could not be minimized anymore, the cost of insurance became dependant on the cash values???

Finally the advisor admitted that he sold the illustration of 6% without the client knowing what he would choose as an investment. In fact, the funds were put in the daily interest account until he made the decision. When the client decided to invest into a bond index, the advisor was obligated to redo the illustration at 4% (with MER, 7% total rate of return). This would have shown the client that for an upside of 1% over the interest rate guarantee of the contract of 3%, he was taking too much rich for little rewards.

Mentioning these facts could have changed the judge decision as to the prescription of this lawsuit. The client paid more than 64,000 $ for a very flawed expertise.

LOBBYING BY INSURERS

"Corporate lobbying by insurers have only one purpose and it is to preserve the status quo by stopping any changes to insurance laws. Looking at how insurance laws have remained unchanged in the last 40 years, I would call this an immense success." (Richard Proteau)

Everyone I have interviewed regarding the insurance industry has described this industry as the old Far West run by cowboys… How is it possible for the insurance industry to exist using commercial practices made illegal in other parts of the financial industry? If a practice is illegal in the mutual funds industry, should it not be illegal in the insurance industry?

The reason is simple. Insurers have the most powerful lobby in Canada and therefore have direct access to all politicians at the federal and provincial level. In three years of advocacy I have not found one willing politician who would be courageous enough to stand up to the insurance lobby. If a politician is willing to listen, it is quite clear that he will be unable to comprehend to scope of the problems existing in the insurance industry as shown by this letter of the Premier of Saskatchewan:

October 1, 2014

Richard Proteau
(rproteau@consumerights.ca)

Dear Mr. Proteau:

Thank you for your email dated September 16, 2014, regarding consumer protection in the financial serves industry. In particular, I appreciate the information you have provided in section one of the Financial Services Consumer Alliance report, as it addresses an important and timely subject.

There can be no doubt that financial services, such as the insurance industry, are key sectors in our economy. Notwithstanding this fact, it remains important to maintain a careful balance in the regulation of this sector to ensure the protection of consumers. Individuals and businesses deserve to have access to high quality, dependable financial services and, as a government, this is a matter we take very seriously.

Saskatchewan financial services legislation is regularly reviewed to ensure that it is functioning properly and serving the needs of businesses and consumers alike. Since 2012, a number of legislative and regulatory amendments have been made as a part of these efforts. For example, amendments passed in 2013 to *The Securities Act, 1988*, established a framework for the regulation of 'over-the-counter' derivatives, which were unfortunately a key contributor to the severe market turmoil in 2008. Additionally, several recent reforms have addressed the way in which pension plans are able to cope in uncertain economic times.

...2

pcu-regina

Richard Proteau
Page 2
October 1, 2014

I hope that your organization will remain engaged in projects respecting the protection of consumers in the financial services sector and I look forward to the results of your work.

Sincerely,

Brad Wall
Premier

cc Honourable Gordon Wyant, Q.C.
Minister of Justice and Attorney General

Honourable Ken Krawetz
Deputy Premier and Minister of Finance

The insurance lobby is also very powerful because of the existence of many groups that act as proxy for the insurance companies. This gives the impression that there are many different organizations providing different point of views on insurance. However this is not the case. Yes, there are many organizations but they all represent the position of the insurers or in this case the position of the Canadian Life and Health Industry Association (CHLIA). Organizations supposedly independent from CHLIA are the Society of Canadian Actuaries for example. Since most of the actuaries who are member of this society are employees of insurers, their recommendations would never be different than CHLIA. You have other supposedly independent organization such as Advocis or Cailba… who position themselves as being independent but will not adopt any stances contrary to the wishes of the insurance.

As a result, when the government is considering a change and request comments from these various organizations, the government believes it is getting various point of views when it is getting one point of view only. This point of view is the insurers' (CHLIA) point of view as shown in this email of CAILBA:

From: Info <info@cailba.com>
Date: Thu, May 8, 2014 at 3:50 PM
Subject: RE: CAILBA Member Communication - Life Settlement (Viatical) Schemes in Canada
To: Daniel Kahan <dekahan@gmail.com>, georgepolzer@islsp.org
Cc: Allan Bulloch <abulloch@ppisolutions.ca>, Arnold Scheerder <arnolds@rgpafin.com>,BobFerguson bobferg2000@yahoo.com>, Casey Brandreth <casey@daystar-financial.com>, David Stewart <david.stewart@financialhorizons.com>, info@cailba.com, Marc Lantaigne <Marc.Lantaigne@financialhorizons.com>, Michael Williams<mwilliams@bfgon.com>,NatalieHo<natalie.ho@logiq3.com>,Nick Simone <nsimone@qfscanada.com>,Paul Brown <PBrown@idcwin.ca>,TerriDiFlorio <terri.diflorio@hubfinancial.com>

Dear Daniel,

Thank you for your query. CAILBA members act as intermediaries for insurance companies and as such, will adopt no stance different from that of insurers. It is not our intention to weigh in on this topic. Rather, our bulletin to members was intended to alert them to the potential for fraud.

Best regards,

Michael Williams

Michael Williams | CAILBA | President | 105 King Street East, Toronto, ON, M5C 1G6
416-548-4223 | www.CAILBA.com | info@CAILBA.com

Consumer protection agencies

It is interesting that no consumer protection agencies want to tackle the insurers and their commercial practices. We have questioned the Union des consommateurs and they have responded that they don't deal with insurance and we have also questioned FAIR which have responded that they don't have enough resources to look at insurance. However FAIR just received $300,000 from Manulife. This excuse is therefore not relevant anymore. If FAIR accepts money from insurers on behalf of consumers it cannot ignore insurance anymore unless this money was paid to get FAIR to look the other way. The answer will come from FAIR actions in regards to this book and whether it will condemn the commercial practices of insurer that are described in it.

From: Jessica Chen <jessica.chen@faircanada.ca>
To: Richard Proteau <richard_proteau@yahoo.com>
Sent: Thursday, September 13, 2012 11:00:08 AM
Subject: RE: Investors rights in the insurance industry...

Dear Mr. Proteau

Thank you for your email and for your support for our organization.

FAIR Canada is aware of the lack of consumer representation with respect to life insurance product regulation. We have made submissions to the Financial Services Commission of Ontario ("FSCO") in response to their Draft Statement of Priorities in 2012 and in 2011 regarding this issue of concern. We noted in our comments that consumer representation is presently lacking and recommended the creation of a consumer panel similar to the Ontario Securities Commission's Investor Advisory Panel, with funding so that it can conduct research and provide written comments.

FAIR Canada does not have the resources to expand its mission beyond securities regulation to also be the voice of consumers in insurance regulation. Given resource limitations, we must focus on our existing strategic priorities.

We encourage you to provide your views on insurance regulation to the appropriate regulators and governmental departments. We would be interested to receive a copy of your report on the commercial practices of life insurance companies, once it is made public.

We believe that you raise a legitimate concern regarding switching clients out of segregated funds (if they were suitable products for the individual to be in) and into mutual funds without the investor being made aware and understanding the consequences of doing so. We suggest that you raise this concern with both the insurance regulators and securities regulators (along with the Joint Forum of Financial Market Regulators) as, in our opinion, it falls within each of their mandates. We suggest you write to the Canadian Council of Insurance Regulators (the "CCIR") and individual insurance regulators (such as FSCO in Ontario) advising that the replacement of segregated funds with mutual funds should be subject to a process similar to the replacement of life insurance (which has recently been revised and changed in Ontario) (as suggested in your comments below). We suggest you also write to securities regulators and the relevant self-regulatory organizations (in particular, the Mutual Fund Dealers Association of Canada ("MFDA") and recommend that mutual fund registrants should also be required to determine whether they are complying with their suitability requirements in recommending the sale of a segregated fund and the corresponding purchase of a mutual fund (in substitution for the other investment product) (again, as suggested in your comments below).

We hope that our comments are helpful to you. We wish you the best of luck in raising the issues you have identified.

Kind regards,

The Team at FAIR Canada

FAIR Canada Newsletter
October 2014
FAIR Canada Announces Corporate Donations

The Canadian Foundation for Advancement of Investor Rights (FAIR Canada) today announced that Manulife Financial Corporation has committed to provide FAIR Canada with a donation in the amount of $300,000 payable over the next three years.

In accordance with FAIR Canada's corporate donation acceptance policy and at Manulife's request, the donation is being made entirely on an arms' length basis and without conditions.

Ellen Roseman, Chair of FAIR Canada's board of directors, conveyed the organization's appreciation, saying "We are grateful to Manulife for its willingness to provide us with financial support and I extend a sincere thank you to Manulife on behalf of FAIR Canada's board."

FAIR Canada's executive director, Neil Gross, echoed those sentiments. "We're tremendously pleased to have Manulife as a leading corporate supporter," he said. "With this very generous donation, Manulife has shown its strong support for a principled approach to policy development through constructive input from all sides. This approach leads to better policy outcomes, benefitting both the investor community and the investment industry. FAIR Canada congratulates Manulife for having the vision and the sincere desire to foster this alignment of interests."

In addition, FAIR Canada today acknowledged receipt of a substantial donation from Talisman Energy Inc., also made without conditions.

"We appreciate Talisman's generous assistance. It's wonderful to see that leaders within companies like Talisman and Manulife support the work being done by FAIR Canada and want us to be able to continue," said Roseman.

FAIR Canada announced the launch of its sustainable funding campaign in April 2014. Commencing with a groundbreaking $2 million endowment from the Jarislowsky Foundation and additional funding from the Ontario Securities Commission and the Investment Industry Regulatory Organization of Canada, the campaign seeks visionary individuals, organizations and companies to establish a broad base of support for FAIR Canada's work.

CONCLUSION

"IT IS NOT THE ROLE OF THE AMF TO VALIDATE THE LEGALITY OF THE COMMERCIAL PRACTICES EMPLOYED BY THE INDUSTRY…"
Jean St-Gelais, president of the AMF April 2007

To which Richard Proteau answered:

"When laws are a convenience for some and an obligation for others, there cannot be a just society; there cannot be a lawful society; conditions necessary for consumers to have confidence in the free market."

ABOUT THE AUTHOR

Richard Proteau has worked in the financial industry all of his professional life. After earning different financial industry designations such as FLMI, CLU, RHU, and CFP, Richard wrote many articles regarding fiscal laws pertaining to investments and life insurance. His last professional position was as Vice President of sales in the province of Quebec for a large insurance company. He has been a speaker at many industry conferences.

He is currently involved in the financial industry as an advocate for the consumer rights of investors and insurance policy holders. Richard is currently lobbying for changes to regulations pertaining to life insurance in order to break a legal status quo of 40 years imposed by insurers in order to protect their illegal commercial practices.

Richard is working on submitting a report on the commercial practices of insurance companies. The first important conclusion of this report is that insurance companies have monopolized the influence over the decisional process regarding the changes needed to modernize regulations in this industry. The consumer is not represented at all. This is why he is one of the founder of the Financial Services Consumer Alliance.

Richard Proteau is also a writer. Having been published in various magazines such as Marketing Options, he is currently writing a fact based work of fiction about fraud in the Canadian financial industry.

information can be obtained
CGtesting.com
he USA
26030417
V00035B/1418/P